Getting Threw

A Story of Survival

WENDY ROSENBERG

To Donna —
a real sweetheart
Wendy

Dedication

To my sweet, beautiful, loving, Charlie and Maurice.
I hope you are frolicking together, over the rainbow with the breeze on your faces.
You will be in my heart, soul and spirit eternally. You are my treasured heroes.
Thank you for almost 18 years of love, and helping me get through!
I love you both now and forever.

CONTENTS

Introduction

Acknowledgements

More Acknowledgements

Introduction

I guess one might think I mistakenly misspelled a word in the title, but getting threw is exactly what happened. I was thrown into a spinning vortex and an abyss of unbelievable devastation, yet through a miracle, I survived. For what seemed an eternity, my life as I had known it ceased to exist. I became an enigma, wrapped in a conundrum, controlled by unknown entities, barely existing in a dream state. I was helpless and immobile, forced to watch and participate in a nightmare of endless challenges. Pain, illness, and isolation became my world. I was compelled to retreat into the inner sanctum of what was left of my spirit and soul where there seemed to be no way out. My heart and mind lay hidden deep in my psyche as if encased in steel armor, exiled in a protection so impenetrable and untouchable in order to enable me to stay safe from the rage of the storm enveloping me.

Perhaps no one would care to hear my story. However, as part of my ongoing healing process, I must tell it so I can free myself through a catharsis, purging the hopelessness and despair I have felt for so long. For anyone to progress in life, there needs to be a separation from that dark place that can hold us hostage. It is a place of fear and defeat where we succumb, and no longer believe in the future. In this place our faith becomes enshrouded in oblivion leaving us with nothing to hold on to.

I still have a long and difficult road ahead of me. However, I am comforted to believe that within us all there is a spark of light, an energy that can stay aflame in the slowly fading embers if we choose to fight with tireless determination and tenacity. It is no easy task, and takes an enormous amount of will to persevere and emerge into a sense of peaceful exaltation.

Against all odds and medical predictions, I am still here! Every day is an uphill battle, an unending responsibility to rebuild and honor my spirit, my very being, and I am committed to doing so.

We all need to draw strength from somewhere, whether it be solely from within or with the help of outside sources. Before surrendering to the hands of destiny, one might consider the power of the human spirit and the exponential force that lies within our own free will.

Acknowledgments

Any traumatic or difficult journey is a daunting challenge, and I must add that without the love, unending attention, encouragement and devotion from my husband Jeffrey, my son Jason, my mom Frances, and my dogs Charles and Maurice, I do not believe that I would have survived.

A very special thank you to my dad Lou, who now has passed on, but remains deep in my heart and soul forever. I constantly feel him nourishing my spirit with strength, and guiding me somehow to never give in or give up.

Thank you all for helping me GET THROUGH.

The First Signs of Illness

In 1967 I was seventeen, living at home with my parents in The Bronx, New York. I dropped out of high school not knowing what I wanted to do with my life. I was somewhat of a rebel child looking for something, although I didn't know exactly what. School was boring, so I decided to venture out into the "real world." I got a job at a private psychiatric hospital in Manhattan as assistant to the chief administrator. It was exciting to feel grown-up and independent. Riding the subway was an experience in itself. Being among the throngs of people from every walk of life, my heart beat in tandem with the cacophony of the sights and sounds surrounding me. I always wanted to be involved in the medical or psychiatric field so this job was a good place to start. On breaks I spent time talking with and reading to some of the patients, truly enjoying the interactions. I realized there was much to learn from people who had been through difficult situations. They seemed to possess a profound understanding of life as opposed to those who had skated through without a scratch. After a year, I realized I needed to go back and finish high school. I took night classes while continuing to work during the day and graduated with honors.

At the same time, I started to experience severe pain in my chest that traveled up into my jaw and down my left arm. It felt as if an 18-wheeler had crossed over me. At first I ignored the symptoms, but as they started happening several times a week, I became concerned. My initial trip to the doctor left me thinking it was my imagination after he told me it was nerves and I had nothing to worry about.

I never considered myself the nervous type, but I thought he was the expert and must know better. We are raised believing that a person with a medical degree is all-knowing so we should trust their judgment and abide by their recommendations. As time went on these episodes grew more intense and lasted longer. I experienced pain so fierce it took my breath away. I wondered, "Could this really just be all in my mind?"

Within a few weeks my mother took me to see another doctor who also told me "it was nerves" and suggested I see a psychiatrist. He said that young women often experience these "anxiety symptoms" so I shouldn't spend too much energy worrying about it, and an antidepressant or tranquilizer should help. I began psychotherapy and started on medication. Months went by, my pain continued, and I began experiencing low moods and apathy. I decided to stop the medication. Within a week or so I felt like myself again!

My mother remained concerned that my episodes showed no signs of slowing down. Another problem arose. I began to have difficulty swallowing certain foods and liquids. Mom phoned another doctor and started to explain my situation. After about three minutes, he interrupted her and stated emphatically, "Your daughter should see a psychiatrist, it sounds like anxiety." He did not even offer to see me in person. I assumed this was just the way my life was going to be, so I gave up trying to get help and realized I would just have to bend like a tree in the wind, rather than breaking, and do whatever it took to deal with my circumstances on my own.

Woodstock - An Aquarian Exposition

In the summer of 1969 there was to be a music festival that was billed as "an Aquarian Exposition" consisting of three days of peace and music to be held at a six-hundred acre dairy farm owned by a man named Max Yasgur in the area called White Lake, near Bethel, New York. Because it was not far from our summer home I decided to go. Many musicians were scheduled to perform there, and it was touted as being "the event" of the summer.

I had to convince my parents that since I had been feeling unwell I desperately needed the distraction. Someone I knew, and his wife, were thinking about going, so my parents said that if I had someone there with me, it would be okay. They had a white Volkswagen Beetle. There was barely enough room for the three of us let alone all of our "stuff," but we managed to pack up the car and start our journey to Woodstock.

As we got closer to White Lake, ahead of us we could see miles and miles of bumper-to-bumper traffic. We could not believe our eyes. We came to a standstill. There were what seemed like tens of thousands of cars stopped on the highway, as far as the eye could see. People were outside of their vehicles, chatting, playing music, and dancing in the middle of the highway. Upon our arrival at the festival, we were immediately engulfed in a sea of humanity. There were people of all ages, shapes, sizes and colors. I could hardly contain myself amidst the chaos. There were hordes of people everywhere walking around, setting up tents, singing, dancing stark naked, and just milling around. There were smiling faces all around us, full of love and anticipation. It was a utopian community based on peace and love. We found a nice spot in a cemetery that sort of gave me the creeps, but it was the only area left with open space. We couldn't believe we were there taking part in this once-in-a-lifetime epic gathering. I don't believe anyone realized the enormity of it all. I felt so fortunate to be a part of this amazing experience, aside from enjoying mind blowing, uplifting, and soul-filling music. Woodstock became a significant part of our generation's history. Luckily, my illness episodes were tolerable at the time and I managed to get through the weekend fairly well. It was beyond anything I could ever have imagined. I saw incredible musicians perform, including Jimi Hendrix, Janis Joplin, and Richie Havens, to name a few, who are all now legends of our time. I volunteered to work in the medical tents set up on the property. There were doctors and nurses who volunteered their time to take care of those who were overdosing on drugs or had experienced various other mishaps. I would be starting nursing school in the fall and was thrilled to be able to help out. It was a great learning experience, and a time that I will never forget.

Realizing My Dream - Becoming a Nurse

My longtime desire to be a nurse became a reality
when I enrolled in nursing school in 1970. In the summer of
1971 I decided to work as head counselor at a camp in
upstate New York. I loved working with children and
wanted to spend time outdoors enjoying the fresh air, before
starting school again, and spending most of my time
indoors. There I met my future husband, Jeffrey, who was
the lifeguard. We became good friends. By the end of
summer we realized we were destined to be together. We
each returned to our respective schools for our final year,
were engaged by December, and set our wedding date
following our graduations in the summer of 1972.

Shortly after our wedding we decided to be
adventurous. We loaded up our car with the little we had to
take a road trip, of sorts. We drove south and ended up in
Jacksonville, Florida. A childhood friend of mine lived
there, and we thought it would be a nice place to stay and
begin our lives together. I worked for a while in a geriatric
facility as a nurse's assistant while waiting for my nursing
board results to come through. I got my Florida RN
certification, and applied for an O.R. internship at a local

hospital. I was accepted and started my training. When I was in nursing school I was petrified about doing my rotation in the operating room because, as a child, I used to pass out at the sight of blood. To my surprise, though, on the first day in the surgical theater, I couldn't get enough. I was totally mesmerized by the intricate methods of the surgical team. I was fascinated with the instruments and technology. Seeing the human body opened up, taken apart, and put back together was unbelievably awesome. I was given the nickname "Blood and Guts", "BG" for short.

I had to arrive at the hospital around four a.m. to start preparing for the day's scheduled surgeries. Although there was so much involved in this process I found it all incredibly stimulating. Each surgeon had his own music genre that he listened to (at that time all the surgeons were male). This was very serious business and an integral part of the morning activities prepping the O.R. We were to cue up the music early so the docs could approve the playlist before beginning surgery. There was much ado and conversation around the operating table despite the serious nature of what we were doing. I would have thought that when life was so critically in the balance, there would be less lightheartedness. However, it was exactly what broke the tension and allowed us to carry out the difficult task at hand.

Jeff and I enjoyed our time in Florida but started to feel homesick after ten months, so we decided to return north to be closer to our families. Our lives felt full, but there was always the nagging of my periodic episodes of pain and difficulty eating. I started waking up in the middle of the night with a throat full of burning acid accompanied by pain so intense I could hardly breathe. There was also the familiar heaviness in my chest, but it now sometimes felt like a swarm of hornets stinging me. I did the best I could, and even had a number of semi-normal days where I was functional, but being so far from loved ones made the bad days all the more insufferable.

In order to break up the long journey home, we stayed with Jeff's aunt and uncle, who also lived in Florida, for a few days. One night, at dinner, Uncle George, a retired dentist, looked at me and said, "You are pregnant!" Jeff and I looked at each other and laughed out loud. Where did that come from? Uncle George then said with a serious face, "You'll see!" The next day we were on our way and kept laughing about the night before and Uncle George's strange prediction.

4

Jason Arrives

Once back in New York, we found a little apartment
in upstate New York, about 65 miles out of the city. We
settled in, relieved to be near our families. I started feeling
tired most of the time, and slept often. We thought this
probably was due to the tedious trip home, but decided it
would behoove us to make an appointment with a doctor
and make sure it wasn't anything to be concerned about. I
had a thorough exam, and the result confirmed I was indeed
pregnant. We couldn't believe our ears. Imagine that,
Uncle George was right! We were ecstatic about having a
baby and couldn't wait to tell everyone. We phoned Uncle
George immediately, and told him that he must have
psychic powers. I don't think I have ever been so excited in
my life. Just the thought of bringing a person that we had
conceived out of love into our world was beyond anything
imaginable. I was bursting with joy and anticipation.

I loved being pregnant, and I embraced the idea of
becoming a mom. I did, however, feel exhausted most of the
time because my blood pressure was extremely low, and I
was unable to work or do much of anything for most of my
pregnancy. In the last trimester I spent a good deal of time

in bed. I realized I needed something to occupy myself.

As a child I always wanted a dog, but never was able to have one because we lived in an apartment and my parents were not keen on the idea. I decided to go to the local shelter and adopt a puppy. I took my mother-in-law, Shirley, and we spent quite a lot of time playing with the dogs. I spotted a sweet little tricolor Border Collie sitting back in the corner of his cage looking fearful and dejected. He was adorable and had the eyes of an old soul. The attendants told me he was found on a country road, abandoned. I was outraged that someone could leave this beautiful helpless little being to fend for himself. How could people be so thoughtless and cruel? I went quietly and sat next to him. He looked up at me, crawled into my lap and made himself comfortable. It was love at first sight and I was not going to leave without this little guy. We brought him home and I went back to bed with our new puppy in my arms. He seemed to settle in and be very at ease with me. When Jeff came home from work, he was surprised to see the tiny furry face peeking out from under the blankets. We named him Samson because he had so much strength behind his shy big brown eyes, and he became an integral part of our family for many years.

My episodes continued sporadically throughout my pregnancy, but they mostly were tolerable. Our son Jason was born in February of 1974, and we settled in to a very satisfying life together enjoying our role as new parents. I was a proud stay-at-home mom and was diligent about providing a natural and loving environment for our son to grow up in.

5

Confirmation of Sanity

In early 1975, my pain returned with a vengeance. I was unable to keep most foods or water down. It was time to seek medical help again. I found a gastroenterologist, Dr. F., at a local hospital. After hearing my story, he said he would like to take some tests. WOW! What a concept. I finally had found a doctor who actually listened and took me seriously. He did not mention nerves or anxiety. He said there were several unpleasant tests he wanted to perform that would hopefully give us some answers, the first of which would be an endoscopy. Under twilight sedation a flexible scope would be lowered into my esophagus that would enable him to see exactly what was going on. Before being sedated I remember thinking that I didn't even care what or how bad the diagnosis would be, I just wanted to confirm that I wasn't crazy.

When I awoke after the procedure, Dr. F. came in to my room, sat down with Jeff and me, and explained that my esophagus was badly damaged. He said it was "fire engine red with severe hemorrhagic esophagitis." There was extensive fibrosis (scarring) rendering the walls of my esophagus fragile and paper thin. He was extremely concerned about my condition, and appalled that no one ever had diagnosed me properly before. He remained positive and supportive and went on to explain that acid from my stomach had been backing up into my esophagus for a very long time corroding the lining due to a serious condition called reflux esophagitis. He felt strongly that if this had been caught and treated years ago when my pain first started, much of the damage could have been prevented.

On one hand, I was relieved to know I was not totally insane, and that I was not imagining my symptoms all of these years. On the other hand, I was terribly angry that no other doctor had ever taken me seriously or performed any diagnostics, and therefore, I now had irreparable damage. Back in the early 1960s and early 1970s there was no widespread knowledge about acid reflux, also known as GERD, or other similar conditions as there are today. The very people we are supposed to trust to take care of us actually exacerbated my condition. I found it inconceivable that I was ignored and misdiagnosed for a period of seven years. How could this be?

I was put on a strict regimen of antacids and instructed to sleep semi-upright on a wedge to prevent the acid from flowing back up into my esophagus. I had to drastically alter my diet, by avoiding anything spicy or acidic. I was to avoid any form of caffeine, and eat several small meals a day. This hopefully would prevent any further damage to my already-deteriorated esophagus. I followed these instructions emphatically and my symptoms abated.

In early 1976, we relocated to Indianapolis for Jeff's job. We were not happy to move again, especially with a two-year-old, but this was a great opportunity we didn't feel we should turn down. We hated being uprooted, but kept telling ourselves that sometimes change is a good thing. Our families were also unhappy about our leaving but understood. We found a lovely apartment in a complex with many young families like ours. It was lonely initially in our new surroundings, but we quickly made many new friends and adjusted nicely. Several months after our move, however, we went through a traumatic time when I miscarried our second child during my 4th month of pregnancy. This continues to haunt me every day, as it probably will for the rest of my life.

Jason was enrolled in preschool in the fall of 1976. Jeff had to take him to and from school, since I worked as the nursing manager at a skilled nursing facility, and my work hours conflicted with Jason's schedule.

After about a year, I decided I wanted to spend more time near Jason, so I applied for a job at his school.

Although I had no formal training as a nursery school teacher I was able to work by sharing a class with a more experienced teacher. Working with children is quite an experience. They are like sponges, soaking up anything that is put in front of them. It was a great time for me because it allowed me to utilize my creativity and spend time with my own child.

Jason eventually started nursery school, so I decided to go back to work in the medical field. I wanted flexible hours. Therefore I took a job working as a home health nurse doing patient assessments and treatments. I met a lot of people from all walks of life and found it very satisfying.

We bought our first house in the spring of 1978. I never would have thought we would be able to own a home, but here we were, in a lovely neighborhood with an excellent school system.

6

Condition Worsens

My condition worsened to the point where I vomited several times a day. Water wouldn't go down without immediately coming back up, and I had to go the hospital for another endoscopy. They found my esophagus to be completely closed due to a stricture. The treatment prescribed was dilatation, where weighted bags of varying thicknesses filled with mercury were passed gently yet forcefully through the stricture to open it up. This was a high-risk procedure and had to be done with extreme caution since it could cause perforations and bleeding. The technical term for this procedure was Bougienage dilatation. My doctor was skilled and able to correct the problem for the time being. This technique remains one of the more important approaches to this vexing problem, and has been updated over the years. They now use flexible angiographic guide-wires with balloon catheters under the guidance of fluoroscopy, which is a type of medical imaging that shows a continuous real time moving X-ray image much like a movie. Perforation has become much less of an issue, although it does to this day, remain a possible consequence.

Even though I was proactive about my medical

regime, things were not improving. My stomach felt full all of the time even though I wasn't ingesting much food. It was time to search for a more specialized expert.

My mom's friend worked at a well-known hospital in New York. She knew of a gastroenterologist there, Dr. B., who specialized in diseases of the esophagus. I decided to call him to discuss and confirm my present diagnosis and treatment regimen. He agreed to see me for a consultation. This, of course, meant flying back to New York, but I felt I had no other choice. Immediate action had to be taken.

Upon meeting him we talked at length and he felt it was necessary to put me through a myriad of diagnostic tests again. He would have to perform another endoscopy, and also wanted me to have a manometry test, which is a motility study of the esophagus where a catheter is passed down through the nose into the stomach. Over a period of an hour or so the catheter is then pulled back out slowly in small increments, measuring internal pressures as it goes. The process was difficult and extremely painful.

After the testing was done, Dr. B. discussed the results with me. In his opinion, I had an extremely rare disease of the esophagus called Achalasia, a disorder in which the esophagus is unable to push food down into the stomach. In a healthy esophagus there are peristaltic waves that work to do this naturally. Peristalsis is a symmetrical

18

contraction and relaxation of muscles that promote a wave-like motion to push food along through the digestive tract. Mine had absolutely no peristalsis and the lower portion of my esophagus, the LES (lower esophageal sphincter), was paralyzed. The upper portion of my esophagus was grossly enlarged from being unable to empty naturally for so long.

Dr. B. said my condition was "complex, confusing and circuitous." He explained that I also suffered with peptic ulcerative esophagitis, which is where there are open sores or raw areas in the lining of the esophagus. My condition was severe and very serious. He told me that very few doctors were experienced with or even aware of this disease, and by some stroke of luck he was one of very few in the United States who had expertise regarding this disease. He went on to say that a strange dilemma was that I also presented with a true acid reflux, which almost never accompanies Achalasia, and to have both diagnoses was almost impossible, but this was definitely the case.

I became flooded with emotion, like I was once again swimming against the waves that were the changes happening within me. As a young adult having gone through so much difficulty for so long, and, in the process trying to maintain my sanity, I started to imagine that I must have been dropped off on Earth from my real planet Pluto to pay penance for some egregious act I committed.

Obviously, I imagined, I must not be from planet Earth, because my body reacts so radically to this atmosphere. Oh, I forgot that Pluto is not considered a planet any more after being "de-planetized" by someone or other. I guess I should go back to my original thought that I came from the planet, "Redhead," which is where all the redheaded beings are from. Redheads are a totally separate breed from the rest of the humanoids on Earth, since they seem to have all of the odd, rare, and unusual health issues that no one ever heard of or knows how to treat. I am still waiting for the "Mothership" to come and take me home.

Dr. B. said there was a surgery that normally would be a possible option, but it was drastically extensive and he was not at all sure I would be a good candidate because of the diverse contradicting anomaly of my condition. We opted to monitor my symptoms closely for the time being.

I returned home to Indiana and continued living my life as best as I could, trying to maintain as much normalcy as I could muster with my abnormal condition. I surreptitiously learned to be a master of composure treading through the labyrinth of my multitude of illnesses.

I had seen several physicians while living in Indiana. The first one practically laughed in my face, stating that this condition only happened to "old people." No one seemed to believe that a young woman could have such problems. It was Deja vu all over again. These physicians usually said, "It's nerves, it's depression, get psychotherapy!" One doctor actually told me my condition was quite progressive and severe, and that he believed I suffered from a serious Collagen disease. These are a group of diseases that affect the autoimmune system by mistakenly attacking your body's healthy tissue in the form of inflammation which attacks the connective tissue. He seemed extremely alarmed and made me feel I wasn't long for this world. The conflicting diagnoses from all of the doctors was baffling to me.

Time passed and my chest pains grew in intensity. I now also experienced pronounced spontaneous regurgitation of a whitish viscid phlegm-like fluid when I ate anything. I could barely get liquids down and started choking at night. The constant discomfort was staggering. I was so tired of doctors, hospitals, tests, and being told there was nothing wrong with me, but I had to continue to seek help. I found a doctor who agreed to do a barium swallow at my suggestion. In this test a thick radiological liquid is swallowed, and then monitored by an X-ray machine. We waited over two hours, but the small amount of barium stayed high up in my esophagus unable to pass through to my stomach. The radiologist said this was highly irregular. There appeared to be a stricture again, so I was admitted to the hospital and dilated under general anesthesia. This gave me some temporary relief. It was such a wonderful feeling to be able to eat and drink without throwing up.

By this time I started feeling sorry for myself. I was infuriated by my incomprehensible situation. I thought God must have given one of the workers on the assembly line a break when I came through. How does justice and fairness fit into that scenario? There is the exquisite land of normal, and then there is this place, this life I live that is made up of the toxic waste of my disease. It was a time when I started to truly believe that the universe was betraying me for some unknown reason.

I felt like caterwauling as loud as I could, while looking up into the great expanse of the sky to let the universe know how miserable I was feeling.

7

Feeling Normal

Over the years I had heard about Dr. Henry
Heimlich, who developed the Heimlich maneuver. This is
an emergency technique for preventing suffocation, in which
abdominal thrusts are used to treat upper airway
obstructions, or choking by foreign objects. He is a
renowned thoracic surgeon, who was semiretired, and
dedicated exclusively to research. I thought it wouldn't hurt
to write to him describing my history, and ask him if he had
any recommendations for me. I sent him a detailed account
of my symptoms, the diagnostic tests I had taken, and my
previous hospitalizations. I expressed that I did not know
what to do or who to turn to for help. I mentioned that
everywhere I turned, there were programs on television or
articles in the newspapers about miracles being performed
every day for people with complex problems and couldn't
understand why I could not be helped. I assured him that
my case was indeed unusual and hoped that with his vast
knowledge and experience in this area he might be the one
to point me in the right direction.

Much to my surprise, within a short period of time,
Dr. Heimlich responded personally. He was very interested

in talking to me further and asked that I call to set up a
phone consultation with him. I did so, and after talking
with him at length, he invited me to his clinic in Cincinnati
for an extensive exam and further consultation. This was
done expeditiously since my situation was rather dire.

After arriving at his office he sat down with me and
said he would like to re-test me using his own specialized
methods in order to properly assess the situation.
Afterwards, he told me he wanted to try a procedure called
pneumatic dilatation, and asked if I would be willing to stay
in town and be hospitalized. He explained that he would
place a catheter that had a balloon-type device into my
esophagus, which would expand the constricted area. I
agreed since at this point, I felt I had no other choice.

The following morning I was admitted, brought to the
O.R., and given mild sedation. I still felt very alert when
Dr. Heimlich started to place the catheter down my throat.
I became anxious and asked for more sedation. The nurses
kept telling me not to worry, that I wouldn't remember
anything that was being done to me. I disagreed, and had a
very difficult time with the procedure. I remembered
everything, and it was not pleasant. Actually it was
unbelievably painful, but somehow I endured.

I stayed in the hospital for a couple of days to
recuperate before Jeff and I were able to return home. I had

some discomfort for a few days, but it seemed as though a miracle took place. I was increasingly able to keep foods down without as much difficulty. So this is what a normal person feels like! It had been so long since I felt good, and I savored the feeling. I was truly grateful to Dr. Heimlich for literally rescuing me. It was worth everything I went through.

Not long after seeing Dr. Heimlich, Jeff was promoted and we had to move yet again, this time to Chicago.

"ONE CANNOT THINK WELL, LOVE WELL, SLEEP WELL, IF ONE HAS NOT DINED WELL."
Virginia Woolf

8

Move to Chicago - Welcome to the Windy City

After several trips back and forth searching for a place to live with a good school system for Jason in the Chicago area, we found a lovely house in one of the northwest suburbs. It was across the street from a beautiful park with a community center and pool.

There was much work to be done before moving in, so we hired a friend of a friend whom I shall call R. He was a contractor in need of work. He would stay at the house and replace the old carpeting and oversee other renovations that needed to be taken care of before we moved in.

We had previously driven our car to Chicago, and left it there for him to use during his time there. We then flew back to Indy for the final phase of our move. We spoke to R daily and things seemed to be going well. He was to be there working for approximately two to three weeks.

When we finally arrived, we found our new home in shambles, and our contractor, R, was nowhere to be found. Upon entering the house, the front foyer had about three inches of water on the floor, apparently from a leak in the roof. Everywhere we looked there were scraps of carpet, nails, empty beer cans, pizza boxes, and candy wrappers.

As if that wasn't enough, our classic 1975 Datsun 280Z, the car we had left in his care, was missing. We felt as though we had entered "The Twilight Zone."

As the days went by in our new neighborhood, the stories about R's three-week escapade started to unfold. Our neighbor came by and informed us that we owed her $3,000.00. Apparently R had knocked on her door the day the carpeting was delivered, and in his charming southern manner, talked her into lending him the cash to pay the C.O.D. delivery charge. My jaw practically dropped! Imagine a perfect stranger coming to your door asking for that amount of money. Would you oblige?? I certainly do not believe I would!

About a mile from our new home was a mini-mart that we began to frequent. After getting to know the owner, we found out that this was where R bought all of his beer and party supplies. The owner went on to tell us that the semi-seedy motel next door was where R picked up prostitutes to entertain at our home. WHAT!!!!!!!!!!!!!!! Would this swirling tornado of chaos ever end??

On the day we were to arrive via airplane, R was supposed to have left our car at the parking garage at the O'Hare Airport with the keys and parking ticket hidden under the mat. There was no call from R to tell us which lot the car was left in, and no vehicle to be found. This should have been our first clue. We had to take a limo home and immediately called the local police to find our car. R, of course, was unreachable.

When the police finally got back to us they said that our car had been found abandoned on the highway near the airport, out of gas and full of beer cans. It had been impounded and was presently in a lot on the south side of Chicago.

Our welcome to Chicago was auspicious, to say the least. All was not lost, however, as we did eventually get our car back and our roof was repaired. It is real situations like these that help make life interesting and enable us to have memorable stories to tell.

Over the next ten years our lives had ups and downs, but we settled in, met new friends, and loved living in the Windy City. My health issues were ever-present and ever-changing. My esophageal problems were status quo, but bearable after the pneumatic dilatation done by Dr. Heimlich.

9

Close Call and a Puppy

In 1983, I suffered a slight stroke and was hospitalized at a local university hospital. It was a frightening time. At one point my parents were called in the middle of the night and had to fly out from New York because the doctors felt I would not make it to the break of day. They arrived at four a.m. to spend what was thought to be my last hours. Guess what!! Somehow, I got through it and lived to tell this story.

The myriad of tests that were done during this hospitalization showed that a blood clot had traveled from my heart to my brain which caused the stroke. Luckily, it was mild and I was left with only minimal consequences of temporary slurred speech and muscle weakness for which I had to stay in the hospital for a couple of weeks and go through innumerable therapeutic treatments. In reading the MRI and CT scans, the doctors also discovered that I had a rare congenital deformity in my brain called Arnold Chiari Malformation. This is an abnormality in which part of my brain called the cerebellar tonsils, extends out of the base of the skull into the upper spinal cord unprotected. This abnormal herniation is thought to be congenital, and may very well have been what had caused all of the migraine headaches and other related problems I had suffered with since childhood. Neurosurgery was highly recommended, but I declined to the chagrin of the doctors. I felt that since I have lived this long with this anomaly, why put myself through brain surgery with who knows what other complications that might arise. Lucky me, I had another "rare" condition! I was eventually released and again tried to live my life as normal as possible.

As a distraction, we decided to look for a puppy to bring some joy into our lives. I have numerous allergies, so we searched for a breeder of Standard Poodles as they do not shed and are known to be hypoallergenic. When we had our adored Border Collie Samson, I suffered with asthma because of his shedding, so we did not want to have that be a problem again. We found a breeder about an hour's drive from our home, and ventured off to pick out our new family member. We met the breeders and were impressed with them and their dogs. The mom and dad who came from a long line of champion show dogs were on the premises for us to see and interact with. The puppies were beautiful. After about an hour, Jeff, Jason, and I selected our new puppy. Jason, filled with tears of joy and excitement held him in his arms on the way home. We named him Bronx Rochambeau, after the area where I grew up. We could not have picked a more loving sweet being. He was black as coal with big brown expressive eyes that melted our hearts. He was rambunctious, playful, very loving, and extremely smart. He was pure joy in every sense of the word and sated our every expectation and more.

We made many good friends over the next few years, and enjoyed our lives. I worked as a hospice nurse, and had to carry an "on call" beeper. I was called out on many occasions in the middle of the night. I was extremely invested in helping my patients and their families go through their sometimes horrific and trying times. It was difficult and exhausting, but most often truly rewarding. I stayed in touch with many of my patient's family members for several years, and received many letters from them expressing their gratitude for my help. One of these letters that touched my heart profoundly was from the son of a patient whom I spent a lot of time with. He wrote...

Dear Wendy,

Words cannot begin to say how I feel toward you. If there ever was an angel it is you. The help and comfort that you were to dad in the final days and hours can never be replaced or thanked for enough.

You were the apple of mother's eye, and believe me, that's no easy position to gain much less keep! God knows Wendy you deserved it!

Please take care and always continue to be the loving and caring person that you are, but don't forget how important it is to love and care for yourself.
Peace and God's speed, Michael

Fortunately, I was able to deal with my own ongoing medical dramas, and focus on helping others, which helped give me much strength and courage.

Jeffrey traveled a lot of the time for work, so Jason and I kept occupied with field trips for school, art projects, and other interests. As a family, when Jeff was able to take time off, we traveled as often as we could. We went to Hawaii to see the Humpback Whales, and visited Epcot Center in Disney World. Jason became obsessed with other countries, so we decided to take him out of school for eight weeks and traveled throughout Europe. We visited cities in Italy, Switzerland, France, Austria, Luxembourg, and Belgium. We did not have a lot of money then, so we spent most of our time staying at inexpensive pensions with local families, and spent many nights sleeping on trains using our Eurail pass, or camped at different sites we were fortunate to find. We were able to experience many wonderful adventures together as a family.

Suffice it to say our ten years in Chicago were interesting and busy.

10

Move to Connecticut

In 1990, Jeff was offered a new job, and we were again in a situation where we had to uproot our lives and move, this time to Connecticut. Although we loved our life in the Windy City and were not happy about leaving our home and friends, we felt it would be a good opportunity for our family.

Connecticut was not as welcoming as Chicago had been ten years before. It was a difficult adjustment period for Jason and me. Jeff liked his new position and adapted immediately. Jason was unhappy about having to start in a new high school at age sixteen, but eventually did blend in and make new friends that he is still close to. He decided after graduation to move back to Chicago and attend college there for one year, but then transferred to a school in New York City where he graduated in 1996 with a Bachelor of Fine Arts degree.

I, though, was miserable and had a difficult time adjusting to our new life during that first year. People were not very friendly in the town we lived in, and it seemed to take a while to meet people we could be friends with. I was feeling fairly well and was able to spend time decorating our new home. We had a lovely patio overlooking a large hill in our backyard, so I decided to turn it into a beautiful garden. I love flowers, so I went to a nearby nursery and purchased a variety of botanicals, and spent hours each day planting. I put up several bird houses and feeders, to be able to bird-watch in my own yard. I tried to feel at home as much as I could in our new surroundings. We did eventually meet some nice people in our neighborhood who became good friends over time.

Two years after our move to Connecticut, our beloved dog Bronx became ill suddenly. We took him to the vet in the morning to see what the problem was. In the late afternoon, we received a phone call that they had put him down because he had inoperable prostate cancer. No one even called to warn us or give us any options. We heard only, "he is gone." Jeff and I were in shock, never having expected to hear such devastating news. Earlier that day we had driven to the veterinarian's office for our appointment. Before going inside we sat on the lawn with Bronx and played with him for about a half an hour so he would have some fun and feel safe before going in for his exam. In my bank of memories I recall it was a beautiful day. The sun was shining and there was a cool refreshing breeze. Bronx was eight years old but still as playful as a puppy, running around with his tail wagging, licking our faces, and being as loving as always. Before we left him in the hands of the doctors, we hugged him and told him we would be back soon to pick him up and take him home, never imagining that we would not get the chance to say goodbye.

Where these veterinarians got the nerve to just automatically put our sweet dog to sleep without a warning was beyond our imagination. I haven't gotten over it after all of these years.

11

Facing Death and Continuing Illness

Not long after we lost our beloved dog Bronx, my dad became ill. I found myself traveling between Florida and New York to help my mom care for him. We went to a multitude of doctors but no one could figure out what was wrong with him. What else is new! The oh-too-familiar enigma syndrome took over. He went through several hospitalizations and tests, none of which gave a clear diagnosis. It took about three years to finally find out that he had kidney cancer and lymphoma. The last year of his life was very difficult. He weathered chemotherapy and other grueling treatments.

Dad had always been a tall, strapping, handsome man, but as time went by, the chemo started ravaging his body and spirit. It destroyed his healthy cells as well as the cancer cells. He became barely a shadow of himself. His weight loss was significant, and he could hardly stand on his own two feet. He had always been a very proud man, but lost himself in the wake of his illness. My mom and I spent many months trying to keep him as comfortable as possible. He and I spent much of our time talking about our lives and the good memories we shared. We also talked about death, and facing it with dignity. His wish was to travel back to his home in upstate New York so he could die where he felt most comfortable. He loved Florida but New York was where his roots were. I had to make special travel arrangements with the airlines. I reserved a row in first class so I was able to care for him without worrying about other travelers being in our way. Mom had to travel in coach, but this way she was able to rest on the way home. It was a tedious trip, but we made it okay. Unfortunately after finally arriving home, Dad's condition worsened and we had to call an ambulance to take him to the local hospital. Mom and I spent the next several days and nights in the hospital with him practically full time. When he started slipping away, I told him it was okay to let go, that he would forever be a part of all of his loved ones. His breathing deepened, and a tear rolled down his cheek. There was a slight hint of a smile on his lips as he took his last breath and gently passed away in my arms. It was one of the most ethereal and peaceful moments I have ever experienced. I then walked out of the room and passed out cold on the floor. My dad was one of the most special people in my life, and he will remain in my heart and thoughts always and forever. I went through a very difficult clinical depression for many months after his death, because I felt an overwhelming and devastating loss with unbearable sorrow shattering my heart.

It was not a good way to adjust to a new life in a new town. I had moved from a home I loved, lost my sweet dog and then my beloved father.

To add to my situation, my esophageal problems started to return with a vengeance. It was difficult to swallow foods again and my abdominal and esophageal pain was becoming intolerable. It took quite a while to find a doctor I felt comfortable with. I did, however, finally go to a gastroenterologist who was very concerned and referred me to another doctor more knowledgeable at a prestigious university hospital nearby. An appointment was set up, and after a couple of meetings, we agreed I needed to have another balloon dilatation done. This university hospital was and remains to be an outstanding medical facility, and Dr. T. had an exemplary reputation.

Upon my arrival at the hospital, I went through the protocol of admission and was brought to the area outside the operating theater. I had to wait for over an hour until I was brought in for the procedure. There was much ado in this hallway. With loud voices and people milling around, this was not a relaxing environment for someone about to go in for surgery. The environment should be a calm and peaceful place where nervous patients could be put at ease instead of being made more anxious. Again, it never seems

38

to be about the patient, only the routine of the doctors and the hospital.

Once I was inside the O.R. the nurses inserted an IV and we waited for the doc to come in. They started infusing the sedation, waiting for me to be knocked out. When the doc began to place the scope in my mouth, I said "Wait! I am not anywhere near out of it."

The nurses said "Don't worry, it will take effect soon." "Soon," though, was not happening at all. I was wide awake! It was deja vu from when Dr. H. did his procedure a few years back. My arm was aching terribly, and I kept trying to tell them that I thought the IV had infiltrated, but they would not listen to me. I had to yell and tell them to stop the procedure and look at my arm, which was indeed quite swollen, turning red because the needle apparently was not in the vein, and the fluids were actually being absorbed into the muscle. The doc seemed angry with me because I was allegedly holding up the works. He didn't seem to care that I was in a lot of pain and my arm was triple its normal size, and it was not my fault that the IV had been incorrectly inserted. They had to disconnect the IV, and the procedure was discontinued. Needless to say my confidence was lost, and I would never go back to have this procedure done ever again. Even the "best" doctors and hospitals seem to have their priorities screwed up.

I began experiencing increasing pain, and started to lose weight. I was vomiting immediately after eating, and feeling terribly uncomfortable all the time. This continued for a long while, and I started seeing many different physicians until I found the right one, or so I thought.

There is a musical group, Belle and Sebastian that Jason had told me about who I listened to constantly. My favorite song of theirs is called "Fox in the Snow." The first line is "Fox in the snow, where do you go to find something you can eat, 'cause the word out on the street is you'll go starving." I totally identified with this song and felt as though it was somehow written specifically for me. The words were a downer, but the song had an upbeat tune that helped get me get through my misery for a while.

I saw many physicians over the next few years, none of whom I was impressed with. I kept thinking about the terms "health care" and "medical care." They both should relate to a person's health and well-being as in treating a patient as an individual. It should not be a-one-size-fits-all scenario. These days like our fast food culture, doctors tend to look for quick fixes and struggle-free solutions to what ails us. Taking medications is not always the answer as they may cause more severe complications than our original problem. Doctors should take the time to evaluate each patient as a human being, an individual, not a commodity.

We are all so different physically, mentally, emotionally, and spiritually, yet most doctors treat us without bothering to take the time to truly know who we are and what our specific physicalities are. Many of them are too eager to put us through needless tests, hand out prescriptions, and quick fix everything. We as individuals must learn to ask questions and be our own advocates. This is ESSENTIAL!!! Doctors are not gods! They are not always correct. Most of us should realize that we are the ones in tune with our own bodies and are often right about what we are experiencing. Whatever happened to the concept of finding out why we have this or that problem or illness and trying to figure out the correct treatment that is best for each of us as an individual? Doctors need to learn to work alongside their patients, and listen carefully to what we tell them. Putting a bandage on a cut does not necessarily take care of the problem. Sometimes if the proper treatment is not used, the cut can fester and become infected.

12

Family Additions

It had been six years since our loving dog, Bronx, had passed away and not a day had gone by that I did not miss him terribly. I had endless memories of his magnificence, his unconditional love and bright spirit that filled our every day with joy, never thinking I would ever be able to replace him.

One day a friend of mine came over to tell me she saw an ad in the newspaper about a breeder of Standard Poodles who just had a litter of puppies. She thought it would be good for me to go look at them on the off chance I would consider owning a dog again. She knew I had been feeling down and said, "Why not at least go and see them? It would be good for your soul, and who knows what would come of it? The poodles are red, a rare color for this breed. Since you are a redhead, maybe it would be fun to see them." After thinking about it for a while, I asked Jeff if he would want to go, and we decided, "Why not?" We did not think we wanted another dog at this time, but it would be fun to at least look at the litter. We made an appointment to see them. There were fourteen puppies, all absolutely adorable.

There were two litters about two weeks apart. The breeders had the parents on the premises, the dad and two moms. The dad was as red as an Irish Setter. One mom was white and the other was apricot. They were well-tempered and beautiful. The puppies ran around and jumped on us with tails wagging. Jeff asked me how we would even begin to pick one out. I decided to sit on the ground and whatever pup crawled into my lap, he or she would be my choice. After about a minute this little cutie sauntered over and climbed into my lap, licked my face, and fell asleep, just like Bronx did so many years ago. It was love at first sight. He was the runt of the litter and had a little white spot on his chest unlike all the others who were solid red. I was hooked. My heart sang with joy, and a deep connection was made. I later found out that his birth date was the same as mine so this had to be kismet. I decided that this would be the perfect opportunity to get two puppies since they were so adorable, and it would be lovely for them to grow up together. Jeff was not thrilled about the idea, but he gave in. We looked at all the other puppies to see who else we would take home. They all had a letter marked on the inside of their ears to identify them. We played with the remaining pups and picked out one marked E. He seemed to be the largest pup of the two litters. They were only a few weeks old and not yet ready to take home so we told the owners we wanted these two males. Over the next few weeks we visited a couple of times a week to spend time with our new boys so they would get to know us. Having fourteen puppies around you is the most amazing feeling. Seeing these adorable furry creatures play together was sheer joy.

When the day came to take them home, we were filled with excited anticipation. A few of the pups had already gone to their new homes, but there were still about ten left. The breeders were busy with preparations so we walked around the grounds. The pups were running around in a fenced-in area. There was, however, one puppy that seemed to be stuck behind another little fence separated from the rest. I went over and sat down in front of him. He had the most soulful eyes I had ever seen. He stuck his tongue through the fence and licked my face making some guttural sounds as if trying to talk to me. After about one minute I was hopelessly in love. Oh my, now what?? I guess I am going to have to take home three puppies I now thought. I knew Jeff would never go for that. I went back to the house and told Jeff about what had happened, and how I had to have this puppy too. "No way," he said. I did not know what to do.

When the breeders came in to present us with our pups, they were holding two. One was the little guy with the white spot and the other unbelievably was this puppy that was behind the fence, not E. I looked at Jeff and said, "What do we do? We had originally picked out E, but for some unknown reason they are bringing us this other pup." Everything in my heart and soul told me we had to take these two, that we were just not meant to have E. I felt bad about it, but somehow it felt right. We actually went outside looking for E, but he was nowhere to be found. Perhaps he had mistakenly gone home with some other family. I guess it was a sign from the universe.

We brought our two new little boys home and they seemed comfortable settling right in. We talked about many different names, but finally agreed to name them Charles D'Artagnan and Maurice Augustus. These names seemed to have a natural cadence to them. Maurice and I shared a birthday date. I was born in August, therefore Augustus seemed perfect. But Maurice was a name I always loved, so I decided to use that as his first name and Augustus as his middle name. Charles was both pup's fathers name, therefore we decided to name Charlie after him. D'Artagnan was one of the Three Musketeers, and although we had only two pups, we decided, why not? We also felt Charlie seemed like an old soul and a hero, so that was the perfect middle name for him. They were precious, adorable little fur balls, and we loved them dearly.

It was Easter Sunday 1998.

13

A New Doc

I had started seeing a new gastroenterologist who monitored my health issues. He seemed fairly capable in my opinion. I saw him on a regular basis and became somewhat confident in his abilities. My condition had become worse and surgery was his recommendation. Dr. L. said I was a "good candidate" for a laparoscopic Heller myotomy and Nissen fundoplication. These were fairly new procedures and less invasive than the open myotomy of yesteryear where the chest had to be opened up surgically, and recuperation took much more time. This new approach involved specialized video equipment and instruments that allow the surgeon to perform the myotomy through several small incisions, most of which are less than a half centimeter in size. The esophageal muscles are visualized and cut, while taking care to preserve the inner lining of the esophagus.

In the Nissen fundoplication procedure, a section of the stomach is wrapped partially around the esophagus in order to prevent reflux symptoms. Dr. L. recommended a surgeon, and we conferred several times before agreeing to go ahead with the operation. My life at this time was extremely difficult. I threw up whenever I ate, and had frequent ferociously painful spasms in my esophagus. Esophageal spasms feel like fiery steel mesh claws gripping and burning inside the chest. They cause overwhelming suffering. They are often equated to the pain of a heart attack and are very often misdiagnosed as one. They are frequently referred to as Cardio-spasms.

Both docs agreed this surgery would "be the best answer for me," and it was my only viable option at this time. I went through all of the pre-op tests. I had several reiki sessions with my massage therapist, which I felt was a good prophylactic measure, and started to mentally prepare myself for surgery. I was admitted and brought to the O.R. on December 8, 1999. I went in feeling positive, knowing this would be the start of better times ahead and a chance at a more normal life. I knew it would not cure my Achalasia per se, but it would enable me to eat more easily, according to the doctors.

Post-op I was in a tremendous amount of pain and obviously out of it from the anesthesia. I woke up in my hospital room with Jeff by my side. I don't remember much except that I was unable to keep even a sip of water down. The nurses said it was not unusual, and it could take a while to feel better. Over the next couple of days, I showed no improvement. Fluids were not going down as they should have, but the docs felt it was probably due to internal edema. They were not concerned. I was discharged and sent home a few days later.

My first night home, I awoke at about one a.m. with the worst pain I could ever imagine. It was as if I were being stabbed in the chest repeatedly with a serrated knife. I screamed for over an hour and then passed out from exhaustion. Jeff called the surgeon several times during the night and finally, at six a.m. he called back. He told me to take Mylanta or Tylenol. Who was he kidding! It was an excruciating, searing pain. It felt as if something inside me had ripped open. Mylanta seemed to aggravate it even more, and Tylenol did not even touch the pain. The night seemed like an eternity. At eight a.m. we went to the emergency room. An X-ray was ordered to determine if the surgery had been compromised. It showed edema and nothing more, so I was sent home with strong drugs to ease the pain. Luckily, by evening the pain became a little more tolerable.

Several days passed and I was still unable to take in fluids except for a small sip or two. I was very weak and uncomfortable. I phoned the surgeon and he told me "It would take a while, be patient, because it was probably due to edema at the surgical site and not to worry."

A week passed and I began to feel a bit wary of the

situation as there had been almost no improvement. The doc agreed to do another X-ray to help re-assure me that nothing was drastically wrong as I was starting to suspect. The X-ray did indeed show edema. Everyone kept insisting there was no problem. However, at my insistence I met with the surgeon again. He agreed to perform another upper GI. I continued to experience dysphagia, or difficulty swallowing, and was vomiting often. I lost fifteen pounds, and had to be given intravenous fluids several times because I had become severely dehydrated.

The upper GI showed severe edema at the site of the fundoplication resulting in minimal emptying of the esophagus. Not a good sign! The doctor continued to feel it should subside over time and said "At worst it may require additional laparoscopic dilatation."

At my two-week post-op visit we discussed my continuing difficulty getting fluids down and the discomfort I was experiencing. Another upper GI was ordered and showed minimal emptying of the esophagus with only little squirts of barium passing through. The radiologist and the surgeon said this was troubling "in light of the supposed technical adequacy of the operation." They felt that as long as I could stay reasonably hydrated with intravenous fluids it would be worth waiting this out. However, they advised that I have an esophageal dilatation done. I was assured that "one way or another I would be rendered able to swallow again." I was not convinced. I was to call them in forty-eight hours.

There was still no improvement, so I was scheduled for a balloon dilatation under sedation at the hospital. I called the radiologist who was to perform the procedure and we talked at length. He too, felt it would improve the swallowing.

14

More Surgery

The dilatation was unsuccessful and I continued to have marked dysphagia. The report concluded there was a fixed point of obstruction in the distal esophagus and would require a second surgery. Distal meaning the farthest end of the esophagus. I was informed the problem was either scar tissue, incomplete myotomy, or some sort of angulation related to my posterior toupet fundoplication. The docs said it was not going to improve on its own, and a second surgery was the only alternative. Jeff and I met with my gastroenterologist and the surgeon, to discuss my situation. The surgeon looked me straight in the eye and assured me it was a simple setback and he had no doubt whatsoever, that after the second surgery, I would be able to eat and drink again. The plan was to perform the procedure laparoscopically to take down the original fundoplication because it was probably too tight. But there was the distinct possibility of conversion to an operation in which my chest would have to be cracked open and it would then become a more complicated surgery. What choice did I have? Something had to be done and quickly since I had now lost over twenty pounds and was extremely debilitated.

I had no energy and felt lethargic and very weak.

Three weeks after the initial surgery, I was admitted and prepped for surgery again. I remember saying to the surgeon before losing consciousness from the anesthesia, "I AM SO SCARED, PLEASE TAKE GOOD CARE OF ME." He looked back at me without saying a word, and then before I knew it I was asleep.

When I awoke I was groggy and sore. I immediately put my hand to my chest to see if they had to perform an open myotomy. I was relieved not to feel bandages covering my chest. I knew I had just gone through surgery, but it felt as if I had been run over by ten tractor trailers. Jeff was in the recovery room with me and explained that originally the operation was supposed to take approximately two hours, but I was in surgery for over seven hours. Apparently edema was part of the problem, but in the few weeks following the initial surgery, I had developed an extraordinary amount of adhesions (scar tissue) that had totally enveloped my internal organs. They were all stuck together in a massive clump. The surgeon had to literally cut all of my organs free from one another, which took hours of intense surgical execution.

The days that followed were touch and go. I was started on a morphine drip to control the pain. The drip caused my blood pressure to drop dramatically. When the nurse took my blood pressure, she became very concerned because it was so low, and that was quite serious. I was hooked up to a heart monitor and given continuous fluids. My legs were placed in a contraption that pulsated intermittently to keep the flow of blood steady so I would not develop blood clots. My electrolyte values were dangerously low and were replaced via IV solutions. I had an intense headache and was extremely lethargic. I asked to be taken off the morphine drip and put on another medication since I felt it was causing my headache and low BP. I was experiencing constant tremors. My body shook so uncontrollably that I found it difficult to breathe. A blood test showed my potassium levels to be totally depleted and therefore I was given IV potassium. The solution burned terribly while being infused. Unfortunately, I was still unable to tolerate sips of water. I thought, not again after going through all of this!

Being in a hospital is never a pleasant experience. I became dismayed by the lack of personalized care. It amazed me that I had to fill out forms upon forms, answer questions upon questions about allergies, intolerances, and a myriad of other personal information, but no one actually paid any real attention to all of the information. The doctors ordered a liquid diet without carbonated drinks. So why did my tray always come up with solid foods and soda?

I was on a caffeine-free, no citrus diet, so why was I served caffeinated tea, coffee and pineapple chunks? I have always been highly allergic to MSG (monosodium glutamate) which had been noted on my chart in bold red letters. When I called the kitchen to ask what ingredients were in the soup that I was served, guess what? It contained MSG! Why wasn't I surprised? I spoke with the head nutritionist several times, but to no avail. Individual needs? Who was I kidding! We trust and believe in a system that is supposedly there to take care of our well-being, but if we are not our own advocates, we are screwed!

There are so many ways to actually improve patient comfort levels. For example, a simple smile always helps rather than the phony "of course dear, anything you need, dear." There should be a mandatory training program for nurses, aides, and doctors (yes, the gods themselves) to learn to understand each individual patient's needs, humility, and feelings. If a care-giver cannot answer a question from a patient, instead of walking out of the room and making you feel stupid and insignificant, he or she should at least say, "I do not know the answer, but I will get you in touch with someone who does." Whatever happened to the concept of seeing the patient as a whole being rather than just a body lying in a bed? I understand hospitals and doctors are busy, but come on, listening to a patient only takes a minute or two. It would make a huge difference in so many ways to so many people. One of my favorite sayings is, "Be kinder than necessary."

15

Not Much Better · Actually Worse

I was discharged days later unable to tolerate more than a few sips of water. Several days post-op, I was still unable to eat anything solid and was growing progressively weaker. I was assessed by a home care nurse. It was deemed necessary I be put on a regimen of IV fluids at home. I had a port installed in my arm and was given daily liquid nourishment intravenously. I was unable to rally after the last surgery. I continued to lose more weight, felt uncomfortable, and grew progressively weaker. As the days passed the situation worsened, so Jason came home to help take care of me. I was unable to do anything but lay in my bed. My mother came up from her home in Florida to help out, and eventually Jeff had to take a leave of absence from work to stay home to care for me.

We spoke with my doctors several times, but they were no help to me at all. They appeared unconcerned yet perplexed. They said they did all they could which I interpreted to mean, yes they certainly did everything they could to ruin my life! Now they were seemingly apathetic. A couple of months passed and I continued to rapidly go downhill with a twenty-five pound weight loss, lethargy, and blood values well below normal. I could hardly keep my eyes open, and was extremely weak.

We made an appointment to see the gastroenterologist and   surgeon again. I had to be carried into the office because I was unable to stand on my own two feet. After an extensive discussion, they noted I was dangerously depleted nutritionally, and now would require a feeding tube to be able to convalesce sufficiently, to improve my clinical situation prior to a more aggressive surgery! Apparently the only answer at this time was to have an esophagogastrectomy in which my esophagus and part of my stomach would be removed. They explained it was a very complicated and risky procedure, and that the recovery time would be at the least six months to well over a year. They continued to explain that I would not survive if I did not have this surgery.

I just about fell to the ground! More surgery! Why would I do that after they practically ruined my life already? I asked if going to see doctors at a larger hospital in New York or Boston, for a second opinion would be practical before conceding to this drastic measure. The surgeon looked me straight in the eyes with that vapid expression of his and said, "If I didn't think I could do this maybe that would be an option, but I am positive without doubt I will be able to correct the situation." His utter arrogance was exorbitantly palpable.

I looked right back at him and said, "You people have done enough, and there is no way I am going to allow you to do any more. If it is my time to die so be it!" The surgeon showed no reaction to this, so we staggered out of his office. Jeff and I were in utter amazement at the lack of care, understanding, or empathy. He was not concerned or interested in what I had to say in the matter even though it was my life hanging in the balance! This was the last contact I had with the surgeon or gastroenterologist. They did not have the common decency to follow up with me to find out how I was doing, or if I had even survived.

My world was crashing down around me. It was as if the flood gates of hell opened up and were about to swallow me whole. I felt utterly and completely alone in a swirling maelstrom, an emotional tsunami, without any hope of rescue. What was I to do? It was beyond my comprehension that these doctors were giving me no alternative aside from more extensive surgery with only a fifty-fifty chance of survival in my present condition without considering any other opinions. Since this was their only answer, I would not let them come near me ever again. It was inconceivable that I was totally on my own. A shell of numbness surrounded me.

To this day, many years later, I cannot even mention that surgeon's name because it makes me ill to think about him.

16

Hope?

I remembered reading a quote some time ago from a lecture by Dr. Francis Weld Peabody, given to students at Harvard Medical School in 1926, that read: "The good physician knows his patients through and through and his knowledge is bought dearly. Time, sympathy and understanding must be lavishly dispensed but the reward is to be found in that personal bond which forms the greatest satisfaction of the practice of medicine. One of the essential qualities of the clinician is interest in humanity, for the secret of the care of the patient, is in caring for the patient."

Dr. Peabody had presented to Harvard medical students, a series of talks that reviewed the essentials of medical care. He emphasized the humanitarian needs of ill people and concluded that the essence of patient care is actually caring for the patient. This quote first appeared in The Journal of The American Medical Association, and became part of the medical school curriculum. The quote remains as valid and inspiring today as it was so many years ago. It is the most cited and revered article in medical literature. I guess my docs must have skipped that class!

When I arrived home, I collapsed into oblivion for

several days. I was in a state of galactic loneliness, like a child lost in the dark, drowning in my tears, and imagining my life was over. I was angry, depressed, and only wanted to fade away. My strength was totally depleted as was my spirit. I lay in my bed with my eyes closed not wanting to think or speak, my future indistinct. When things are good, hours and days hurtle by in the flash of a heartbeat, but when things are bad, time seems to stand still, obscuring everything. I retreated into the deepest corner of my psyche feeling totally and irreparably derailed from life, like a spent fire that gives neither warmth nor light, indelibly changed. I lost "me" in every sense of the word.

A few days passed and I forced myself to face the reality of my dire situation. I guess in the many hours of silence I found a place where I could listen to my inner voice and it was saying, "Okay, this is it, enough self-pity. No more letting doctors control my life. Trust no one and embrace a challenge. It is time to get it together and fight." Although I was disgusted, in pain, and completely exhausted, something inside made me realize this was truly do or die, and decided at that moment, I was not ready to give in to the fate I had been seemingly dealt. Survival mode seemed to take over insanity, and I seriously began to think about what it was I needed to do to survive. As they say, "It ain't over until it's over!" These universal words of wisdom came to mind. "God grant me the serenity to accept the things I cannot change, courage to change the things I can and the wisdom to know the difference."

I was about to embark on the journey of my lifetime, with insurmountable challenges to save my own life!

I was still only able to tolerate sips of fluid over many hours, which I knew was not going to get me far. I started to research nutritional supplements that could possibly renew and rebuild the strength of my body. Being bedridden, though, I had to involve my family to help me research natural remedies. We purchased a variety of vitamins that I found might be helpful in my quest, and the most nutritious powdered protein drink I could find. I emptied several different vitamin/supplement capsules into the drink and blended them together. I sipped this powerful potion slowly at intervals throughout the day. It was not the most pleasant tasting beverage, but if this was to be my salvation, taste was not a priority as long as I could keep it down. After about two weeks of this routine, I actually felt a slight spark of strength re-emerging in my body. My family told me my eyes looked brighter and my voice seemed a bit stronger. It seemed like a miracle that the potion was working.

In February of 2000, I started looking for a specialist in esophageal disorders. It did not matter where the doctor would be located. I was willing to go almost anywhere, even Europe if need be. I found Dr. K. at a university hospital in Pennsylvania who sounded promising. After several tries, I was able to speak with his office manager and relate my story. The next day I received a call from the doc himself, who was very interested in hearing what I had been through. After our conversation, we set up an appointment to see him in a couple of weeks. I felt I needed more time, though, to gain strength before traveling to Pennsylvania.

I had practiced yoga for many years and always felt it was a great healer. I did not have the strength to actually do poses, but thought that any relaxation technique would suffice for now. Jeff lit candles around our bathtub, played soothing music on a portable CD player, and helped me immerse myself in a hot bath infused with essential oils. I used deep breathing techniques, meditation, and visualization. Closing my eyes, I imagined my esophagus smooth, open, and functioning normally. I visualized healthy cells circulating throughout my body attacking toxic ones. I used my hands, starting at my feet and scanning up through my entire body mentally pushing out all of the malevolence in me. I would then open my arms above my head as if letting the good spirits from the universe seep into my mind, spirit, and body. I visualized beautiful colors surrounding me. I imagined purple, gold, scarlet, and bright pastel lights streaming into my body, healing me. I inwardly asked for whatever good there was floating around in the universe to please help me in my quest for better health. This became a nightly ritual. While it may sound like hocus-pocus to some, I was convinced it was going to work.

Miraculously between my potions and meditative visualizations, I started to feel somewhat stronger. It did not happen overnight, but gradually.

Jeff and I planned our trip to Pennsylvania to meet with Dr. K. It was to take about six hours by car. We packed enough of my shakes so I would have a good supply while I was away. We went with hopes of hearing something we could work with in order to get through the nightmare I had been barely living though.

Dr. K. ran a gamut of diagnostic tests, most of which I had been through before, and the results were compared with past reports and X-rays I had brought with me. He was compassionate, gentle, and caring as a physician should be. He made me feel as if I was the only one on his schedule that day. He listened to my every word intently, never making me feel insignificant. When the tests were completed, he went over all of the results, and quite simply said that my situation was indeed dire. He said that I should be seen and evaluated by an expert. He recommended a doc in California who was world-renowned in this particular field, and who recently had been working on esophageal transplants. Dr. K. called him to make the necessary introductions and arrangements for a consultation whenever I was strong enough to travel. A trip to the west coast was a tremendous undertaking for me at this time, so I had to put it off for now.

But, I would not stay still. I decided to consult with experts a little closer to home. First, we went to see Dr. B. in Providence. He was, "Surprise, surprise!" an arrogant sort of fellow. He was very rough-and-tumble, and not very personable. He told me I needed to have a feeding tube installed immediately, and would most likely never be able to eat again. I decided not to continue with him.

In late February of 2000, we were off to a well-known hospital in Boston to see Dr. M. the division chief of thoracic surgery. Again, the answer was similar. He said I was in no condition to have more surgery at this time. He too, felt I should be hospitalized, and have a feeding tube placed to be able to build up some stamina, and prepare for an esophagectomy (removal of the esophagus), because in his esteemed opinion, I would never be able to eat again without this surgery. I declined.

In early March of 2000, New York seemed the next plausible place to go. We consulted with Dr. S. who was well-known in the field of cardio-thoracic surgery. We brought all of the previous reports, and asked him to review them and give us his opinion. He was nice enough to spend a lot of time with us and discuss my options. He, also felt I was not nearly stable enough to go through another surgery at the present time, and should wait at least six months to be reevaluated. He recommended that I prepare myself physically and psychologically for an esophagectomy and colon interposition once I was able to gain some strength. Although he wished me luck, he did not offer any constructive ideas or hope.

17

Coping Better - Slowly Getting Stronger

Over the next several months I struggled each day to cope as best as I could. I sipped my potions, meditated, visualized, and kept a positive attitude. I said to myself that I will get through this and come out the other side strong and healthy. I decided I needed to start opening the locked doors in the long corridors of my mind, body, and spirit, and find myself once again. I needed to break out of the shell I was enclosed in and be reborn in a sense, accepting my fate, and rebuild the shattered wreckage I had become. I embraced a mantra that I repeated several times a day, "May the white light of the universe surround and protect me." I allowed myself to think only positive thoughts, never letting my spirit fall too low, or give in to negativity. I started journaling about all of the things for which I was grateful. This was difficult since I was not feeling very grateful at the time, but I realized that when we look deep within ourselves there is truly always something for which one can be grateful. We must focus on these things no matter how small or inconsequential they may seem. Getting through each day was a major challenge. Being unable to eat like a normal person and being unable to socialize or partake in everyday activities was unbearable. Most of all, being a person who had always been in charge and having taken care of everyone else, I now had to succumb to others taking care of me. It was an abandonment of self to give up all control. That was the most difficult task for me. Somehow, ever so slowly, little by little, time passed and things started to improve somewhat. Those who are blessed to be able to live fairly "normal" lives cannot fully comprehend how very difficult life could be under these circumstances.

By September of 2000, I was feeling that perhaps I would be able to travel to California, so I called Dr. DM. to set up an appointment.

18

California Here We Come

I scheduled an appointment in October of 2000. Jeff and I left for Los Angeles. By this time I had gained more strength thanks to my homemade potions, and felt fairly comfortable making the arduous trek across the country, even though I would be going way out of my comfort zone. We decided that after what I had been going through, we would do it first-class all the way. We upgraded our airplane seats to first-class, booked a room at the five-star Ritz Carlton in Pasadena, rented a luxury car, and looked into some interesting tourist sites we would enjoy. Although I would be spending most of my time at the hospital going through difficult tests, we also wanted to have some fun things to look forward to.

Upon our arrival at the magnificently posh hotel we were informed that an error had been made and our reserved room was not available. Unfortunately the hotel was totally booked. The manager came over to us. He appeared utterly and completely mortified and apologized profusely. He said he would accommodate us immediately, but it would not be the same type of room we were expecting. We were exhausted after the long trip and just wanted a comfortable bed to rest our weary bodies. We hoped the room would not be substandard. The manager asked that we follow him out of the hotel. He took us by car to a property on hotel grounds away from the main building. We had no idea what was in store for us. We drove up to a beautiful cottage that appeared to be a single family home. When we entered, our jaws dropped! This was no ordinary place. It was rambling and opulent! There were three bedrooms, a fully-equipped kitchen, a dining room, and a huge living room. It was absolutely gorgeous, and had every amenity one could imagine. We felt like royalty. The manager said he hoped this would be to our satisfaction. We stood aghast, unable to speak. He smiled and said to call him anytime if there was anything else he could do for us. What a lovely surprise!

The next day we drove to the hospital to meet with the big-time doctor. He seemed nice enough for a world famous specialist, though mostly clinical. For the first test, I was to eat part of a hamburger that was laced with nuclear medication. These few bites were to be monitored radiographically traveling through my GI system. I was only able to tolerate a small bite though which lodged in my esophagus unable to go through to my stomach. The next procedure was endoscopy under sedation, followed by manometry. It took some convincing by the doc for me to go through this test again, but he assured me it was imperative. I asked to be given a sedative, but I had to be alert and unmedicated to get an adequate reading. I won't go in to detail, but suffice it to say this was by no means pleasant, and that is putting it mildly. We were to return the following day for the results.

The next day our meeting was informative to say the least. Dr. DM. told me I was in end-stage Achalasia with a massively dilated esophagus, due to a stricture at the lower esophageal sphincter. He also said that the surgery I had months before was definitely incomplete, and actually seemed to be virtually non-existent. He continued to tell me that he could not identify any repair whatsoever when he had scoped me and, at this point, after two similar surgeries, it was too risky to re-operate. In his opinion, a total esophagogastrectomy, removal of the esophagus and stomach, was my only option at this point, otherwise my chances of survival were not favorable. Well, I thought, thank you very much. Been there, done that, don't want any part of it!!!!

Who we are as individuals, how we see ourselves, and what we feel is right for us, should be determined by ourselves and not by others who may or may not be invested in us. It is said, "At the dawn of every morning hope springs eternal." I must force myself to continue to believe that.

Jeff and I left the doctor's office frustrated and confused but here we were, our first time in Los Angeles, and I was not going to let what had transpired ruin it for us. Yes, I was feeling devastated again, but I put on my happy face and forced myself to enjoy the time we had left in California. I would save my grim and miserable pity party for when I got home.

We visited the Gamble House, which was amazing, and the Getty Museum which was candy to our eyes. The following day we went to Santa Monica and drove the Pacific Coast Highway and Mulholland Drive to glimpse the famous Hollywood sign. We walked Venice Beach, and strolled around the beautiful town of Pasadena. A shopping tour on Rodeo Drive was an experience in itself. Luckily I had the strength to do it all without problems.

It was around dinnertime so we went into a lovely little Italian restaurant. I was unable to eat solid foods at this time so I asked for a soda and slowly sipped while Jeff ordered his meal. Our waiter kept rattling off all of the delectable items on the menu trying to entice me to order something, but I insisted I was not hungry. He kept coming over to us putting his hands in prayer position with tears in his eyes saying, "I worry for you, Senorina. You are so pale and thin, you need to eat a good meal. Let us make something special for you. We can make anything you desire." I did not want to get into a long complicated conversation about my condition, therefore I kept insisting that I was not hungry and would be fine. He was very sweet.

It was time to get back to reality and prepare for the long trip home. We packed up, said good-bye to our beautiful cottage and California, hoping to return again someday when I was well.

It is impossible to articulate how truly devastated I felt as the mounting frustration and disappointment welled up in me. I knew I had to stay focused and continue on my quest for answers.

19

Consequences of Life Changes

It is very interesting to me that when my life changed dramatically and I was no longer able to keep up with the everyday activities of life, people I thought were my friends slowly started to disappear. Some stuck with me no matter what but many did not want to be bothered or burdened. I found it very unsettling that people stuck around when I was well and "normal," but when things got the least bit messy I seemed to fall off their radar, hence the lyric by the incomparable John Lennon, "Nobody loves you when you're down and out." Some people actually became annoyed that I wasn't my "old self." It didn't happen right away, but gradually as time went by. I know this may seem unbelievable, but I can assure you it can and does happen. One example were family members we had entertained for many years at Thanksgiving. I spent countless days and hours preparing and cooking the annual family Thanksgiving feast. The year I couldn't host this event, these particular family members stopped calling or caring, apparently because I was unable to continue this tradition. They seem to have felt slighted that I stopped inviting them, never even bothering to ask why or investigate further.

Many people I thought were my friends eventually stopped calling and coming around, saying they just did not know what to say or do. They felt helpless. Instead of trying, they seemed to feel it was easier to ignore what was happening to me and disappear, like stopping at the gate instead of walking down the bumpy road. Some people were actually angry with me when I said I could not go to restaurants anymore. They felt I should at least sit with them at the table while they were eating, even though I could not partake in that traditional ritual. Would you ask a sightless person out to enjoy a beautiful sunset? Would you ask a hearing impaired person to listen to a symphony? I think not! One friend actually had the nerve to tell me I should be grateful I didn't have cancer and to just get over myself! It was unbelievable, but true. I guess she automatically assumed I did not have cancer.

I had to liberate myself from the expectations of others. I had too much to deal with in my everyday struggle to put any of my strength, little as it was, into worrying about others. I felt hurt and alone, but tried to push aside these feelings, not letting them get me down any further than I already was. I could not understand how people could be so shallow and let fear, or lack of understanding, negate friendship. I often felt invisible, incomplete and minimally existent like a shadow or a vapor. It felt as if I had no impact in the world. I felt like I was becoming ghost-like, fading away, barely existing in this activity called life. As the amazing Carole King once sang, "When you're down and troubled and you need some loving care, and nothing, nothing is going right... They'll hurt you and desert you and take your soul if you let them. So don't you let them."

Whatever happened to...
"Ain't it good to know that you've got a friend!"

I have unfortunately learned all too well about so-called friends and finding out who matters and who does not. True friends are rare, rock steady, and salt of the earth. However, those who gave up on me, of which there were many, I named Cloud Jumpers. They were here one minute and vanished the next. A very famous man once wrote, "Be who you are and say what you feel because those who mind don't matter, and those who matter don't mind." Dr. Seuss.

But I digress.

20

Hope Rises - Again

At this point I had seen more physicians than any human being should in a lifetime. I just wanted to make sure I knew all of my options. I now felt I needed to continue doing whatever I could to gain strength and heal on my own. It was time to look for a general doc who could oversee my everyday well-being. I interviewed several. Many said there was nothing they could do for me and actually did not even want to take me on as a patient because my situation was too complicated! That certainly made me feel better and reassured!! I had seen a total of six internists and had one more to go, although by now, I was about ready to give up. After each failed interview I sat in my car and cried, feeling so very alone.

I decided to go ahead and finish what I had started. The last interview was with Dr. G. and I was prepared to hear the same scenario, "Sorry but I cannot help you." We sat in his office and I related my story to him. He seemed to be a kind and gentle man, listening without judgment or concern of time passing. He actually became teary-eyed. He stood up, moved closer to me, and embraced me like a lost child. He then sat me down and took my hands in his, telling me that he too probably was unable to fix my problems, but absolutely would be able to help me through whatever came up, whether it be referrals, tests, or medications. He told me he would monitor me in any way possible and be available in whatever capacity he could. He would be my advocate. I practically collapsed in his arms with sudden relief, finally feeling that here was a kind and caring individual who took the time to listen and actually care. Dr. G. was about to become my hero.

The years 2000 and 2001 were difficult ones. Getting through each day was indeed a challenge, trying to adjust to life as it now was for me. I did not partake in any meals, and had to sequester myself in my bedroom while Jeff ate alone. It was too painful to be near the aromas and sight of food. I couldn't watch TV because every other commercial was about food, which upset me terribly. Unless you have been banished from eating, you cannot even begin to imagine how devastating it is not being able to taste any of the delectable delicacies that other people enjoy and take for granted. It seemed to me that the majority of people live a fairly normal uncomplicated life. They go about their daily regimens of reading the morning paper, having a cup of java contemplating what their day will be like. Shopping, lunching with friends, chatting about trivialities, or taking a leisurely walk. I know there are a vast number of people with many unfortunate and varying degrees of illnesses. Yet, the majority of people take the apparently "normal" activities for granted. It may not seem like a big deal, but when so-called routine things are off limits, one cannot imagine the impact it can have. I remember riding in the car going to my doctor's office noticing a woman walking down the street with a cup of coffee in one hand and a donut in the other. She seemed to be thoroughly enjoying herself. I was envious and felt immense anger at the indignant injustice of being unable to do such a simple thing. Anger has a way of taking over one's senses. Then I realized I was only hurting myself. Therefore I needed to come back to reality and be grateful for being alive and not let the minutiae consume me.

I was still in a weakened condition so we did not socialize or go out much. I was incarcerated in my small protected world, a victim of my disease.

Beginning to strengthen my physical/mental health and well-being was a constant chore, but one I was determined to conquer. I was still not able to eat solid foods, but I got by, drinking my shakes that constituted my meals throughout each day. I was tolerating them more readily and taking larger amounts than mere sips. Imagine not being able to eat anything for months! One would think that is impossible, but amazingly, many things are possible if we change our mind-sets. I remember someone telling me she could not live without this or that favorite food. But, I am a true example that one certainly can do without quite a bit in this life if one focuses the mind to it.

My strength was gaining momentum as was my compulsion for life, as if I were beginning to emerge from my chrysalis. Not a day went by that I was not grateful for seeing the new light of every morning. I forbade myself to be negative in any way, even in the face of so much adversity. It sometimes seemed impossible to face each day while being totally cut off from the real world. I knew I had to endure and force myself to have the courage of my convictions to stay strong, no matter how difficult it seemed. I was determined to prove all of the doctors wrong and get through this seemingly impossible scenario. I kept telling myself there is no pit too deep that I cannot climb out of.

21

Ways to Cope

There are so many different ways people suffer in life. Pain, illness, or isolation, to name a few. Who is able to say which is worse? Only the one going through the suffering can say for certain. There is no better or worse, more difficult or easier, in suffering. There are no instructions, exams, or grades in this subject. Somehow people who go through life without adversity cannot seem to grasp or understand how impossible getting through can sometimes be. They tend to judge, label, and deny without fully understanding. On the other hand, animals seem to be more able to feel and fully understand the human spirit. They sense the inner workings of us humans, and they feel the pain and suffering on a basic innate level. They give constant and unconditional love without any expectations in return.

My dogs, Charlie and Maurice, for example, were always by my side sensing my every mood no matter how insignificant. Any time of day or night, the moment I felt the least bit uncomfortable or down, they were by my side in seconds. They seemed to know my every thought and truly kept me grounded through the ever-changing landscape of my life.

Some caring friends invited Jeff and me to their home in the summer of 2001 in order to get us out of the daily grind of being stuck in a routine of misery. I had not been out in a very long time, and after much deliberation decided it would be a really good thing to visit them for a change of scenery. There would be no pressure of a meal or any activity, so why not? They said, "We'll just sit and enjoy one another's company." It was a lovely day and off we went. While sitting in their screened-in porch, I suddenly found myself saying, "This is the way I would like to be living." Their home was out in the country, wooded and secluded. We listened to birds chirping their melodious songs like an orchestral piece, watched frogs croaking while sunning themselves on lily pads in the pond, and heard the sound of the breeze gently whistling through the trees. I never cared for the neighborhood we were currently living in and had always wanted to move to a remote location amid nature and all her glory, where the din and clamor of life would be less intrusive. Thank you, Carolyn and Joel, for this special day.

On a whim, I started looking through the newspaper for a home in that town. After all we had gone through, Jeff and I both thought it could be a possible new direction for us. Lo and behold, like in a dream, I sighted a small two-line ad in the real estate section advertising land for sale in that very neighborhood. Perhaps, it was a sign from the universe?? We made a few calls and went to see the property. As we drove up to the area a strong feeling developed in the pit of my soul. When I stepped on to the land, I knew I was home. There were twenty-eight acres of woodlands that were to be divided into five lots. It was a very secluded, serene, wooded expanse high up on a mountain. We walked around and picked out the lot that we felt would be best for us.

We went back to the lot several times to be sure this was really *THE* place, and each time we were more convinced that this was definitely our home to be. We spoke with the developer and put down a deposit to purchase the land.

22

A Day That Will Never Be Forgotten

Early in the morning of September the 11th, 2001 I had an appointment at the eye doctor for my yearly exam. As I was leaving the building to go home, I overheard two people talking about a plane crash in New York City. When I arrived home I immediately turned on the news. It was the beginning of probably what was to be one of the most horrific days in our lifetime. The Twin Towers were hit and malevolence and mayhem ran amok. I could not believe my eyes and ears that such a nightmare was taking place. I immediately called Jason, who lived in lower Manhattan, to see if he was okay. I was unable to get through since the lines were completely blocked, and I became overcome with panic. Shannon, a close friend of his and mine who lived nearby me, showed up at my front door. She was terrified and did not want to be alone. She knew I would be frantic and wanted to keep me company. We sat and watched together as the unimaginable drama unfolded before us. We were in a state of shock as was most of the world. All I could think of though, was hearing Jason's voice, and know he was away from the danger. Not until late in the day did I hear from him, and he told me he witnessed the entire scene up close. He actually watched people jumping from the windows of the Towers. I need not go into the details of that day since everyone knows it all too well, but I felt beyond blessed that my Jason was safe. We did, however, lose two dear friends who were in the Towers. They will remain in our hearts forever. I love you Shanny, and thank you for being my rock that day.

23

The Letter

I kept myself busy designing our new home. Anyone who has ever been involved in the construction of a new house knows it is not an easy task. Is anything in life?? I was gaining strength and was able to do more and more. Miraculously, after all of the doctors told me I would never eat solid food again and presumably left me for dead, I came back better than I ever thought possible. I was eating, although on a fairly restricted regimen, and beginning to enjoy life anew, except for a constantly nagging, coarse feeling about the doctor who performed my surgeries, and had made my life a living hell for so long. It was the second year anniversary of my surgeries, and I felt that in order to let go of the anger and resentment I had been dragging around inside of me for so long, I had to put it to rest by writing a letter to him, mailing it, and then getting on with my life.

I wrote this letter and sent it to him:

Doctor------,

It is amazing to me that after all the time that has passed, I am still unable to say or write your name without feeling ill. What is interesting to me is that you probably never even spent one single minute of your time thinking about me and possibly don't even remember me.

Today is the two-year anniversary of when you first operated on me. An "easy, practically risk-free surgery" it was supposed to be. My life was to be so much better after this surgery, "a much improved quality of life," to quote you. Well, two surgeries and two years later my life continues to be a living HELL, and I owe it all to you. I have endured months of pain and debilitation. I have had to travel around the country in search of someone who could help me after what you did to me. I have been to NYC, Boston, Rhode Island, Philadelphia, and California, seeing the supposed top surgeons and physicians in this field, all of whom agreed that I might have had a fighting chance, if only you had stopped after the first surgery and sent me to someone more qualified and experienced in esophageal diseases, not to mention the difficulty of traveling in my fragile condition, or the exorbitant expense of it all. At this point it is unfortunately too late, and I may never again be able to function as a normal human being. My only option now, according to all of these doctors, is to remove my esophagus and part of my stomach, and go through more pain and suffering with a minimal chance of survival. Being in such a debilitated condition due to the two surgeries you put me through, I would have to wait at least a year to even be considered a candidate for this extensive surgery.

When I last saw you it was in your office and I was rapidly declining, but your answer at that time was, "The only thing left to do is remove your esophagus." How stunned I was that was all you had to offer. If I let you proceed I have no doubt I would now be deceased.

Many times after our last visit, I contemplated taking my life. My pain, discomfort and frustration was devastating, plummeting me into a severe clinical depression. I was given absolutely no cooperation, care or compassion. You were of no help at all, which left me feeling totally abandoned and alone. I started out a vibrant healthy young woman, but thanks to you I became a very angry, bitter, sickly being. Instead of my quality of life being improved, it was completely and utterly devastated. So many times during and after the surgeries, I desperately tried to tell you that something was very wrong, but you refused to listen to me. You kept insisting that my problem was caused by edema and it would resolve itself. You really should learn to listen to your patients instead of letting your mega ego be your guide.

I thankfully, was eventually able to take matters into my own hands, slowly researching everything and anything that would build my strength back up after being unable to

even get out of bed for six months due to extreme weakness.
My husband and son had to take extended leaves of
absences from their jobs to stay home and take care of me. I
won't go into the details of my semi recovery with you since
I am sure it is of no interest to you whatsoever, but I felt in
order to heal, my first step was to write this letter and bury
the heavy boulders of anger I have been lugging around for
two years.

I have been trying to deal with the deep anger and
hatred I feel towards you that has consumed me for so long.
Not only for what you did to me, but the unmitigated gall of
you never having the common decency to follow up on my
status. You mangled my insides and evaporated my faith in
life itself. I ask myself over and over, how someone like
yourself could cut open a body, changing a life in an instant,
and never even take the time to care enough to find out
what became of that person.

I had occasion to laugh (something I rarely do these
days) when I saw your smiling face on the cover of
Connecticut Magazine as a best doc in Connecticut. I
laughed so hard it made me cry for hours, after reading your
words of how important patient care was to you. How could
you have said that with a straight face? What patient care?
I never had the pleasure of experiencing it. With me, it was
just rip her open and leave her to die, never even bothering

to look back and wonder.

I remember asking you before the second surgery, if I should go to someone else more experienced in this field, and your exact words were and I quote, "If I felt I could not help you, I would send you to someone else, but I am positive that I can have you eating and feeling well in no time." What a mistake it was to trust you.

I would like you to try to imagine never being able to taste all the delicious wonderful foods most people enjoy on a daily basis. Never being able to enjoy the simple treat of going to a restaurant. At every mealtime, having to leave the room because it is so difficult to watch others eat, and not be able to smell the aromas because it is too painful. Being unable to socialize with friends or spend quality time with family. Of course if there was a plausible reason for this I could somehow deal with it, but the only reason I had, was that you, my doctor, who I put my trust and faith in, did something to me that was definitely not right, and caused this to happen. Food is the primary source of life. Every magazine you open has advertisements and pictures of glorious food. Almost every television commercial is about food. Most conversations between people start and end about food. I have spent the better part of the last two years relearning how to live without that marvelous staple of life. I truly feel that you are the one who single handedly

took this necessity and pleasure of life away from me
because you did not care enough to understand my disease
and treat the matter more professionally. I was just
another body you had to cut open and experiment with.
You, who are touted as being the best surgeon in this area,
should be ashamed of yourself for being so uncaring and
giving such poor patient care, or should I say un-care?

I could go on and on about how my life has changed
and what a living Hell it is and how much hatred I feel
towards you, but that would only be a waste of my time, and
time is something I have learned is so very precious and
treasured. I guess I just needed to let you know that a life
you touched has been destroyed, and hope you might spend
a minute in your busy day feeling sorry about it.
I don't know what else to say.
Wendy Rosenberg.

I sealed the letter, put it in the mailbox, and tried to
close that chapter of furious anger that was taking up too
much space in my life.

24

Our New Home

In April of 2002, we broke ground and started the construction of our new home. Fighting with the builder and contractors became my world for the next several months. All in all it took the better part of a year, but it was well worth it. We moved into our new home on Christmas Eve, December 2002, when our vision became a reality. The first thing we did was go to a nearby farm and cut down a Christmas tree. Before unpacking, Jeff, Jason and I spent our afternoon decorating our new tree. We listened to our favorite holiday music, and enjoyed the afternoon in our new home together, celebrating life.

One of my life long dreams has always been to live on a lake. At this time in our lives though this was not possible, so for now I thought I could at least be near some water. I decided to design and build a beautiful pond on our property, with six waterfalls and a flowing stream.

One might wonder how I muster up the strength to do what I do at times. I continuously strive to deal with my ever-present health issues. I am not the type of person to let life pass me by. If I am able to get up and move around, I push myself past any limitations whenever I can. I never let my pain and weakness get the best of me if I can help it. Some days are just easier than others to do so. When I have a day that the pain does not paralyze me, I try with a vengeance to grab life by the horns and live to the best of my ability. I have been told by many of my doctors over the years that I have an incredibly high tolerance for pain. I truly believe that if I set my mind to it, I can do almost anything, under any circumstances! That is just the kind of person I am, and I am very grateful for that! I do not believe in the word impossible. Most things are possible and attainable if you set your mind to believing that.

The plan was to add gardens and make our backyard a natural habitat for birds and other creatures. I had gone back to school a few years before to earn my Master Gardener degree. Therefore, I had some knowledge of how to beautify our surroundings. Little by little over the next few years, I immersed myself in spending six to eight hours a day designing and planting our gardens. It was very healing, and I loved having my hands in the soil. It made me feel part of something very special. My mind and spirit were where my strength came from, pushing me to my limit. Those who plant, endure storms and all the vicissitudes of the seasons. They rarely rest. A garden never stops growing, and while it requires the gardener's constant attention, it also allows life for the gardener to be a great

94

adventure. It was glorious to be so at ease with the land
and feel like a real person again. It was as if I was tilling
and nurturing the soil of my soul at the same time.

In my garden I felt grounded and anchored to the
earth. Being amid the natural world gives infinite rewards,
asking little in return. While working in the garden,
whether it was weeding, pruning, planting, or just being, my
mind, heart, and soul, were nourished beyond my
imagination. The garden always gave back more than I
could ever put into it. It reflected everything beautiful and
pure. The next few years were more enjoyable than the past
few. I had my good days, and my bad days, as many of us
do. Our home and gardens were a constant source of joy
and contentment for me. Having fauna, flora, and an
abundance of various species of birds, frogs, and butterflies
in my backyard, I decided to rekindle my love for
photography. I truly believe that gardening and
photography became my salvation and helped me get
through all of the pain. I spent endless hours looking
through the lens of my camera, clicking away, capturing a
plethora of stunning images of the natural sights
surrounding me. I was drawn in to a world of the sheer
magnificence of nature that kept me sated. Life was
good....... until, it wasn't.

25

Plagued by Symptoms

Late summer and early fall of 2006, I started having a strange metallic, salty taste in my mouth, and thought it must be from something I had eaten. As the days went by, though, the taste got stronger and it began to concern me. I was also experiencing abdominal bloating, which made me feel very uncomfortable. I was under the care of Dr. N., a gastroenterologist whom I was seeing at the time. I found him after researching many different doctors. After speaking with him, I had blood tests taken to see if anything was awry. The tests came back mostly normal except for slightly elevated pancreatic levels and an extremely high B-12 level. An ultrasound showed a gallbladder full of stones. An upper GI showed my esophageal anomaly, but no other suspicious problems were obvious. I had a vague roiling in my gut though, sensing something was amiss.

After discussing the test results with Dr. N. we decided I needed to have an endoscopy. Even after fasting for two full days, the procedure could not be completed because my stomach was full of undigested food. So what else is new!

By January of 2007, the strange taste in my mouth

was continuing, and the bloating was becoming intolerable. Twenty minutes after each meal I felt as if I had swallowed broken glass. It was becoming rather painful, and I was concerned. By early February I started to feel fatigued. I had been losing quite a bit of weight, even though I was eating fairly regularly. I spoke with Dr. N. and told him I did not feel these were my familiar esophageal symptoms, but rather an abdominal issue, perhaps it was an infection. I felt quite sure about this, and asked him to perform another endoscopy, and to take a biopsy while I was being scoped to check for Celiac disease. Bloating was one of my symptoms, which is many times a classic symptom of Celiac. The result showed that my stomach was filled with fluid and left over food that should have been digested days before. There were also numerous polyps covering my stomach lining. These would have to be removed and biopsied.

The next step was to take a test to see if my stomach was emptying correctly. It was now February of 2007. An appointment was set up at a lab. I had to eat a small meal, and then lay on an examination table for two hours while X-rays were taken in order to see how quickly my stomach emptied. This procedure is called a gastric emptying test. I explained to the technician that if I laid down, there was no way the food would travel into my stomach because of my esophageal problems, but he said it did not matter. As expected, nothing moved out of my esophagus, and I was told I had a motility disorder called Gastroparesis. Just another diagnosis to add to my ever-expanding roster of diseases. Lucky me. I guess the disturbers of my harmony are back.

Gastroparesis is a motility disorder. The stomach is a muscular sac located in the upper middle of the abdomen just below the ribs. It normally can stretch to hold approximately one gallon of food and liquid. The stomach folds in on itself when empty and expands when one eats or drinks. Stomach walls are lined with three layers of powerful muscles that mix food with enzymes and acids produced by glands in the inner lining. Once the food is pulverized, strong muscular contractions called peristaltic waves push it toward the pyloric valve that leads to the upper portion of the small intestine, where digestion takes place.

The most important nerve in the body is the Vagus nerve. It stretches from the brainstem to the colon. It helps orchestrate the complex circuits in the digestive tract. When the Vagus nerve is damaged, these contractions slow or stop completely, and food does not move out of the stomach into the small intestine as it should. Damage to the Vagus nerve is one of the leading causes of

Gastroparesis. Operations involving the esophagus, the stomach, or the upper part of the small intestine, can injure the Vagus nerve and lead to Gastroparesis. Symptoms can develop immediately after surgery or several years later.

There was no doubt in my mind, that my Vagus nerve was damaged more than once when I had undergone esophageal surgeries in the not so distant past.

Dr. N. admitted me to the hospital for further tests to evaluate the situation, since my weight loss was significant, about thirty pounds so far. I now weighed eighty-five pounds. While being checked into my room, the nurse said to me she wished she was as thin as me. She was a little overweight, but not terribly so. I looked at her like she was out of her mind, and told her to be careful what she wished for, that she should really think seriously about what she had said. I was emaciated and, did not in my opinion, look very healthy. Dr. N. came in shortly after and told me that I was going to have to finally give in and have the esophagectomy. He said that at this point, there was nothing else to be done. I said to myself, not this again!

I kept insisting this was not my Achalasia, or anything to do with my esophagus, but Dr. N. continued to be his arrogant self-absorbed, condescending self. He looked at me and said, "You know this is because of your esophagus and it needs to come out." After he left the room, I immediately started the process of checking myself out of the hospital. I had had enough with this doctor who was so very full of himself, never listening to what I thought, or had to say. I left his practice and never saw or heard from him again.

Throughout this time, I had kept in touch with Dr. G., as he continued overseeing my care and progress, being my constant mentor. Over the years he gradually became a true and dear friend. Unfortunately, he was having some medical problems of his own and had to take several leaves from his practice, forcing me to start searching out a new physician. This was heartbreaking for me, and no easy task. Dr. G. passed away a few months later. I will always miss him dearly.

During February and March of 2007, I felt continuously weak. I spent most of my time in bed, unable to do much of anything. My pain continued to worsen as the days went by.

In early April of 2007 a friend told me she knew of a doctor in North Carolina who specialized in Gastroparesis. I called and spoke with him. An appointment was set up, and I was to go to the University Hospital where he practiced, for tests and an evaluation.

We decided to drive to North Carolina and make an adventure out of it. We did some research and located a quaint rustic horse ranch that rented cottages equipped with kitchens. That would enable me to prepare my own meals, as restaurants were not an option. This seemed the perfect place for us to stay. The ranch was in the middle of majestic surroundings with beautiful towering mountains and scenery that was breathtaking. As a child I was a blue ribbon horse rider and had worked at a local horse farm near my home. I love horses and thought it would be great to spend time with these magnificent creatures after being in the hospital all day long going through difficult diagnostic testing. Knowing that animals have amazing natural healing abilities, it was an ideal divergence. We took three days for the trip, so it would not be too taxing in my weakened condition. We brought the food I needed in a cooler, so we would be able to eat on the go. The trip was not easy, but as I mentioned before, when I set my mind to pushing myself to do what has to be done, I am able to make it happen.

Winter was just nearing its end. The further south we drove, the more we were able to notice telltale signs of winter edging into spring. As a gardener, I love spring. It has special meaning. It is all about hope and rebirth. Driving under a bright clear shimmering azure sky with floating mother-of-pearl clouds, we noticed trees on the verge of awakening with a burst of tiny buds emerging.

There were hints of luminous cadmium, burnt sienna, and ocher, sneaking out of the ground along the dismal gray highway. This is my favorite time of year, when after a long sleep under extreme conditions, signs of the resplendent brilliance of nature start awakening. A "getting through, if you will" of frigid temperatures, snow, ice, and wind. It has always amazed me that delicate plants are able to survive this long siege, renewed and full of life, starting the cycle anew. Hardy bulbs buried beneath the ground push their way through the soil and begin to display their magnificent profusion. We are not all that different from those gnarled roots and bulbs. They start off small and vulnerable, pushing their way through the dirt and mulch coverings, growing stronger as they develop thorns and thistles for protection. When their season has ended, they fade again, and develop a protective outer shield enabling them to hibernate for the winter, in order to rebuild strength under the dank, dark ground. Then, one miraculous day, they once again start to emerge from the darkness and grow stronger, more fortified than ever. What a wondrous happening to behold!

Dr. K. was personable and showed us around his clinic before I had to start going through the tests he had set up for me. At the end of the day, I could not do very much since my condition was compromised, but I did somehow manage to spend time with the horses, which I found comforting. They are such beautiful, amazing beings, offering comfort and unconditional love. Standing beside these awesome beauties and stroking their necks and faces brought so much joy to my spirit. It was in itself a renewal of which I cannot even begin to express in mere words.

The upshot of the week in North Carolina was that I had Achalasia, as if I didn't know, but the doc did not feel I had Gastroparesis. His opinion was that I suffered with irritable bowel syndrome (IBS), which in my opinion is a popular catch-phrase for any unexplainable abdominal problem. He also said I most probably had severe nerve damage from my past surgeries, and that there were medications I could take for that. I did not have much confidence in his assessment, except for the diagnosis of nerve damage, which I already knew. I felt this was a wasted trip, aside from the time spent with the horses and witnessing the coming of spring. Foiled again! Oh well!

The trip home was lovely, for even after only a week, the magnificence of spring was ablaze all around us. It was good to get home. I had terribly missed my dogs, Charlie and Maurice. I spent the next several days playing with them constantly, giving them both lots of love and soaking up their love in return.

26

Another Gastroenterologist

I thought it would be prudent to find a new gastroenterologist for yet another opinion, so I asked my OBGYN doctor, who's opinion I valued, if she had any recommendations. She told me that her good friend was in the same practice as Dr. N., and she would talk to her about setting up a consultation. I wondered if there might be a conflict of interest, but she said it would not be a problem.

An appointment was set up with Dr. S. in late April of 2007. We met in her office. She sat across from me in her examining room with a very stern serious face and told me she had gone over all of my records. She then went on to say, "I am doing this as a favor to our mutual friend Dr. R., so I will be brutally honest with you. I am here to tell you that if you do not have an esophagogastrectomy you will die." She was very curt and not so sweet. I kept trying to tell her that I felt this was a different problem than my esophagus. The pain was in my lower abdomen, and after forty-eight years of knowing my familiar pain, this was very different. She insisted with her acerbic intonation, it was from my esophagus, because she was the doctor who knew better, and I was only the patient. I asked if she was at least going to examine me, but she said she did not have to, since she knew without doubt, what the problem was. The only option, in her opinion was surgery, and she proceeded to tell me in her churlish way, exuding an air of complete and utter arrogance, how extensive it would be and that the recovery time would be a year or more. She said that if I was even able to survive the surgery, because of the severely de-conditioned state I was already in, I would never again be able to live a normal life. At this point I wondered if I did not know what I was talking about because she was supposed to be the expert, so possibly she was right. It seemed to me at that moment, there really was not much to look forward to or hope for. This doctor was a small, good-looking woman, and according to her, she knew exactly what was going on and she made me feel that I had no right to an opinion, even though it was my body and my life we were talking about. She was extremely unpleasant, condescending, and downright mean. I could not believe the sheer arrogance and evil that emanated from this egomaniacal woman.

I left her office flummoxed and in a daze. I felt as if I had been accosted on some level. I sat in my car for over an hour because I was trembling from the insurmountable fear welling up within me about my indistinct future. I felt tears pressing hard at the backs of my eyes, once again feeling that my world was ending. I felt broken and unfixable like shattered crystal.

While driving home, I decided that it was time to do something drastic. I could not go through this agony anymore. If this surgery was truly my only option, and it appeared that this was indeed the case, I did not want to go on living. When I got home I sat down with Jeff and said we had to have a serious talk. I told him that after all I'd been through, I could not go ahead with this surgery and then be unable to live my life as I wished. I asked him to please understand that I could not go on this way anymore, and I wanted to end my life. I am the kind of person who has always had my hands in a myriad of things, and I did not wish to be an invalid barely able to function. Knowing myself as I do, this way of life, or lack thereof, was not an option for me. I would rather end it now. I was afraid of death, not knowing what if anything would await me on the other side, but this was no way to live either, being in pain and misery all of the time. I barely would be existing. I just wanted to be at peace. I knew this sounded insane, and a lot to take in for both of us. Jeff gently put his arms around me, held me tight, and started to convulsively weep. He looked me straight in the eyes and said, "We have gotten through tough situations before, and we can and must do it again." We talked for many hours, and I promised I would give it some time for all of this to sink in. I was physically and mentally exhausted. I needed to sit back, take a deep breath, and evaluate the situation thoroughly before making such a rash and final decision. I went to my bedroom, collapsed into my bed, and slept for about eighteen hours.

27

To Dr. L. in New York City

We decided to look for an esophageal specialist in a big city, where the doctors perhaps had more knowledge of unusual diseases. New York City was the next likely place. After extensive internet research, I found Dr. L., in Manhattan. He was associated with a prestigious hospital. An appointment was made, and although I continued to grow weaker, we drove to the city to talk with this new doc. He seemed personable and very knowledgeable. We sat in his office and talked for quite a while about my history. I had sent him copies of past tests and reports, so he would be up-to-date about my present condition. He put me through an extensive examination, listened to my opinions, and said he would like to perform an endoscopy/gastroscopy to be able to properly assess my condition. We set it up for the following week.

Simultaneously, I started seeing a new general doctor near home. She came highly recommended by a woman I know and trust, and seemed to be as caring and concerned as Dr. G. was years before. After meeting with her, I felt she would be a good substitute for my dear departed Dr. G. Dr. D. spent quite a lot of time with me at our initial meeting and listened to my story without judgment. She told me that she would do her best to be my advocate, and would help me in whatever way possible. She put me at ease, and I felt extremely comfortable with her.

Traveling back and forth to New York at this time was difficult because of my pain and weakness, but I had no choice. I was now dealing with the "big leagues." I had grown weary of the doctors and hospitals in my hometown and felt my disease was beyond their scope of comprehension. I must repeat that I find that most doctors don't take enough time with their patients, like in the old days, when they actually seemed to care about you as an individual. Many of them utilize what they are taught from textbooks, and don't seem to use their own imagination or instinct to deal with anything that is outside the lines of "the norm." If it is not black or white, like the written pages of a book, they don't seem to know what to do. Gray areas seem to be verboten. They don't know how, or choose not to think outside of the box. If they would take the time to listen to their patients, they might find that they may actually learn something. Imagine that! I guess they have too much pride to wrap their inflated egos around that concept. In my opinion, many doctors, even the caring ones, are limited to a short amount of time to spend with each patient, which truly does not allow for quality care. Every day you hear about mistakes that occur in medicine such as surgical errors, incorrect diagnoses, and many other serious faux pas. Every day, a new medication is being recalled, and attorneys are constantly advertising on television about how patients need to participate in class action lawsuits against drug companies. I remember once telling a doctor that I was allergic to penicillin, and guess what he wrote a prescription for? I believe it is truly unfortunate that so many people are misdiagnosed every day. Doctors more times than not, do not listen to their patient's input, and make snap judgments that often times are incorrect. This is something that desperately needs to be addressed! Too many deadly and intractable mistakes are made on a daily basis and this needs to be rectified!

28

Journaling

I started journaling at the end of May 2007, to be able to have an outlet for my thoughts and feelings, and to keep a record of daily events.

1st Journal Entry May 25, 2007
It is 9:00 a.m. and I am going to try to start journaling. I have meant to do this so many times, so here I go...
Today wasn't too bad a day in the scheme of things. I walked in the garden which always brings me joy. Had an esophageal spasm this afternoon which is my worst pain but I got through it somehow. It lasted about an hour. It is so frustrating to have so many difficulties. NOT EASY BEING ME! I just hope that whatever it is that keeps me going continues to get me through this dark miserable siege. It is time for good things to happen. These last four months have been a total nightmare and I am now due for better times. Here's hoping!

We went back to New York to have the endoscopy/gastroscopy done. It was performed under anesthesia in the operating room. I did not even remember the drive home.

Dr. L. called and said that I had a raging infection in my esophagus and stomach. I was unable to swallow pills or drink fluids. Therefore I had to go back to the hospital for IV antibiotics. The next step was to wait until the infection abated, and then he would perform a balloon dilatation. This was done two weeks later, but was unsuccessful. Dr. L. said that Botox injections into the esophagus sometimes yielded good results, and he wanted to try them on me. It seemed we drove back and forth to Manhattan almost every week for one procedure or another.

Monday June 4 of 2007. We were up at 3:45 a.m. for the drive to the city for the Botox injections. It was done under anesthesia, during the endoscopy.

Journal Entry June 5, 2007
Feeling very uncomfortable, disgusted, and frustrated. Unable to get any liquids down without major problems. Discomfort level high. I have to stay in denial to get through this. This is HELL. I am having a very difficult time coping today. No one realizes how impossible this is. No food for four months. What's the use? I find it unbelievable that there are no answers. I wish I knew what I am being punished for. My life has fallen apart. I don't know how much longer I can keep this up.

The Botox injections were ineffective, and by this time I was beyond exhausted. I was tired of running back and forth to Manhattan. I spoke with Dr. L. and he said I should take a few weeks off, and try to get some rest. This complication seemed to be an unusual result, but hopefully the situation would reverse itself.

The next day, I was unable to get any of my liquid shake down without extreme pain. I was feeling very weak,
112

so we went to our local hospital emergency room. When we got there, I collapsed on the floor from sheer exhaustion. My blood levels were critical, so I was immediately admitted and given blood transfusions.

Out of courtesy, Jeff called Dr. S., the nasty female doctor who told me I would die without removing my esophagus and stomach. He thought he should let her know that I had been admitted to the hospital. Her response in a very truculent tone of voice was, "I told your wife this would happen if she did not listen to me about having her esophagus removed, so there you go" and she hung up. Jeff stood there with his mouth agape, and did not even know how to respond.

29

New IV Lines

I was diagnosed with severe esophagitis and gastritis, and had to stay in the hospital for twelve days. I was fed intravenously, and had to be given several units of blood daily. I ended up having a double TPN PICC line installed. A PICC line is a peripherally placed central catheter which is inserted into the arm. The procedure is done under fluoroscopy for precise placement. It starts in the arm and extends to one of the central veins, such as the subclavian, with the tip of the catheter in the superior vena cava of the heart. Apparently the Botox injections had made matters worse. TPN stands for total parenteral nutrition. The subclavian arteries are asymmetric paired arteries that supply blood to the posterior cerebral circulation, upper limbs, and the superior and anterior chest wall. The vena cava are large veins that return de-oxygenated blood from the body into the heart. Parenteral nutrition is a method of getting nutrition into the body through the veins and or arteries, bypassing the usual process of eating and digestion. This formula contains nutrients such as glucose, amino acids, lipids, and added vitamins and minerals. I was unable to eat or drink anything orally. Therefore I needed to be fed this way indefinitely. When there is total disuse of the gastrointestinal tract, this is how a person is able to maintain nutritional balance. The PICC line is powered by a battery-operated infusion pump, which needs to run for twelve to sixteen hours a day. This allows nutrients to absorb directly into the body. Complications may be many, including bacterial or fungal infections, liver complications, blood-clots, etc.

It took the doctors several days to convince me that this was my only choice to enable my survival. My condition was deteriorating rapidly, and there truly was no other option. I weighed approximately seventy-six pounds and was severely malnourished. One of the doctors, who visited me daily during rounds, talked about my esophageal disease ad nauseam, and kept insisting that I needed to seriously reconsider having my esophagus removed. He was emphatic that I would die if I kept putting this off, even though I continued to insist that I felt that the issue was something other than my esophagus. I was beginning to believe there was an inexorable lugubrious conspiracy to rid me of my evil esophagus. I was in a quandary about what to do.

After three days of the docs trying to convince me that I must have the PICC line installed, I gave in. I was terribly anxious, and asked to be given a sedative before the procedure. A high dose of Ativan was administered through my IV. It helped me relax to the point of being able to tolerate the procedure.

Before being discharged from the hospital, the representative of the home health care agency that was to follow me at home, visited to discuss all of the procedures, processes, and protocols that were to be involved in my care after I left the hospital. There would be an initial visit from a home-care nurse to instruct me and Jeff about the maintenance and usage of all the medications and equipment. There would also be weekly home visits to change my dressings, check my vital signs, and general condition.

Shortly after we returned home a nurse arrived, and we began our initial instructional session. My condition was tenuous at best. I had to be assisted out of bed into the kitchen, where we were to assemble all of the components involved. We needed a large area to work on, so our kitchen table was the most logical place.

There is a plethora of information one needs to absorb about caring for the PICC line. The line feeds intravenously into the heart. Keeping the site and all of the accouterments involved 100 percent sterile is therefore critical. There is a pump, bags of solutions that must remain refrigerated until use, innumerable medications, and nutritional supplements, that all have to be infused into the solutions. There are syringes, IV hookups, and the list goes on and on and on! We also had to inject a medication called Heparin into the catheter, before and after each infusion, to prevent the development of blood clots.

This scenario was akin to a highly intricate procedure that was left to two lay people at home using a kitchen table. The nurse was only there to help us the first night, so we were on our own every night afterwards. We could not even begin to fathom how we would be able to get through this nightmare. When the nurse left, the angst and fear in the room was overwhelmingly palpable.

Every night involved high drama, like an episode of the television series "ER" except there were no commercials to give us any respite. We were both on the verge of nervous breakdowns.

Every afternoon we had to remember to take out of the fridge, a bag of solution at a predetermined time, so it would be at room temperature by evening when we had to measure out all of the various and sundry medications, and ever so carefully infuse them into the solution bag. We then had to thread the tubing through a maze of connections and attach them to the pump, making sure the solutions were evenly dispersed. We had to meticulously and painstakingly make sure there were no air bubbles in the tubing and solution bag, because allowing air into the veins and heart could prove perilous. Keep in mind that everything we came in contact with had to be wiped down vigilantly with alcohol so as not to contaminate anything. Infections are a nasty side effect that one does not want to experience. Once all of this was completed, we had to attach the tubing to my PICC line, turn on the pump, and hope for no major complications. The fluids were to be infused during the night over a sixteen-hour period. There was an alarm on the pump which did go off many nights when air had managed to get into the tubing, which scared the bejeezus out of us. We then had to spend hours trying to clear the lines. NOT FUN!!!!!

An IV stand was set up at my bedside so we would be able to measure out and infuse exact dosages of other medications, separately and with extreme caution and deliberation, such as sedatives and narcotics. These were injected directly into the tubing for a more immediate effect.

These daily and nightly rituals became an endless living nightmare. The consensus of opinion was that I would, without doubt, need surgery to have any chance of surviving. However, I would have to wait several months to gain enough strength to be able to tolerate the radical procedure that was being proposed.

Journal Entry July 7, 2007
Well it has been about a month since last writing and a lot
has happened. Was in the hospital for 12 days. It was
horribly difficult. Discharged with TPN and had to take a
crash course on learning all the meds and feedings to be
done at home. My fear is overwhelming. There just has to
be better times ahead!!! I don't know how to get through
this.
I am trying so hard to be positive in this miserable
situation but it is getting harder. I feel shaky and weak and
am having such a difficult time dealing with the constant
pain.
No one can begin to understand how I have to make myself
go into a void, an abyss, just to get through each day. I have
not been able to eat or drink a thing for over 5 months. I
am literally STARVING to death. How I am doing this
without totally losing my mind is beyond me. People
constantly talk to me about food they ate or recipes they
cooked or restaurants they went to and how delicious
everything was. What the hell are they thinking! Are they
totally clueless??
I have no life, being homebound without joy, just pain and
misery. This just has to get better. The prospect of major
surgery ahead of me is too much to think about, I must take
it one day at a time, too overwhelming!!!
What has happened to me? What has become of me?? I try
to be positive but my strength is waning rapidly. I know I
have gotten through bad times before, and I must find the
courage and wherewithal to do it again. GOD, please give
me strength!!!!!!!!!!!!!

Journal Entry July 9, 2007

Jason home for the weekend and that always makes me feel better. He is just what I need.

I know JR is having a difficult time. His life is dedicated to getting me through all of this. I feel so much guilt that he has the burden of taking care of me.

Nurse came today for blood work and to change my dressing. Counts are down. No wonder I am so tired and weak. The docs seem to be at a loss as to what to do to fix me. I can't seem to get out of bed. I am in so much constant pain. Having too much anger and feeling down today. Have to stay focused and positive, taking one day or actually one minute at a time so I can heal. My situation keeps me in the depths of despair. Cannot let myself feel so hopeless. It is not good for me or anyone else. I feel adrift, unprotected from the deluge engulfing me. Some days there is a blurring of lines between illusion and reality. *HELP ME, PLEASE!!!* Is my trying to stay positive just an exercise in futility??

Journal Entry July 14, 2007

Feeling a bit stronger today. JR and Jason went out for the afternoon at my insistence. They need some respite. They need to get out and do something fun and have time away from caring for me. I know I am not the only one suffering. I guess I am feeling sorry for myself not getting out and having fun too. What is that anyway?? I feel so left out of life. I have nothing to look forward to except surgery that will do who knows what to me? Maybe even end this misery one way or the other. Surgeons don't really care about the quality of my life. They just do their job and that's it. My fears are taking over.

Doc called with blood results. Most are very low and others quite elevated. *NOT GOOD!!*

Very concerned about the future. I don't seem to be getting anywhere and things are so complex. Who knows what the

120

docs will be able to figure out, if anything. They all seem so one-dimensional, not creative at all but here I am, having to trust them.

My life is so miserable, pain too much to bear most of the time. Despair keeps pulling me down deep. I am at a loss as to what to do and finding it more and more difficult to keep my emotions in check. Rage and despair growing and I fear losing control. In a downward spiral into nothingness and I don't want to reach the bottom. No one can even begin to understand how impossible this all is.

I miss my life desperately. Wish I had confidence that things will be okay. The only thing I look forward to these days is getting Ativan to put me out of my misery.

How do I possibly begin to describe what it is like to wake up each morning with a burning in the belly and chest that takes my breath away, being unable to function like a regular person, with weakness that is all consuming? I keep trying to acclimate myself to get through the day with pain that can fell a giant. Denial is a word that comes to mind. Somehow, most of the time, I can mentally transport myself into a deep state of denial and plod through the day. If I am lucky, sometimes the pain ebbs, and I am able to tolerate the discomfort with a modicum of dignity. Usually, no matter how badly I feel, I am able to somehow neutralize it all in my mind, and become an Oscar-winning actress, a seasoned performer extraordinaire, with the amazing ability to fool all of those around me so that no one ever suspects the depths of hell I experience on a daily basis. I have named myself the "Queen of Pain." I am grateful there are times, although most brief, of respite from my agony, and it is those times I covet. I think about people who get up every day without ever a thought of anything but, "What shall I do today?" How I envy those people. I can only dare to dream what that must be like.

By mid-July my condition was no better. Actually, I was continuing to lose weight and grow weaker. After many discussions with Dr. L. in NYC, we decided to speak with Dr. A., a very-well thought of thoracic surgeon at another well-known NYC Hospital. I had to have an endoscopy done again, where both Dr. L. and Dr. A. would be working as a team. Dr. A. wanted an up close and personal look at my esophagus to try to evaluate the situation more realistically. What a concept!! A surgeon no less, who was not immediately insistent on removing my vital organs. After speaking with him at length, he continued to remain unsure as to what would have to be done. He explained that he would not know for certain until he was inside my chest cavity. He said that a total esophagectomy was a definite possibility, but he wanted to assess the true situation, and make his decision based on what he found during the endoscopy. The procedure of choice, if need be, would be a thoracotomy. This is thought to be one of the most difficult surgical incisions to recuperate from because it is extremely painful post-op, and that pain more often than not prevents the patient from breathing efficiently, leading to many pleural difficulties including pneumonia. A thoracotomy is a large incision into the pleural (lung) space of the chest. The cut goes from the front of the chest wall to the back, passing underneath the armpit with surgical cuts between the ribs. He went on to explain in too much detail for my comfort, how very difficult this surgery is to recover from, and would most likely take well over a year. I was surprised and amazed that this surgeon did not insist on a total esophagectomy immediately, like everyone else, and actually admitted that there was truly no way to tell what had to be done until he was able to accurately assess the situation from inside. The picture he was painting for me was clearly not cut-and-dried, nor pretty. I was no doubt in a horribly compromised state of ill health, and my chances of recovery or even survival were not good. There was no choice, however, whether or not to go ahead with the surgery. It was only a matter of time to know exactly which procedure was to take place. We were to meet again with Dr. A. in a couple of weeks.

Never Give In

One day, as I sat in my chair looking out at my garden, feeling oh-so-sorry for myself and crying uncontrollably, I noticed a tiny little frog no bigger than a couple of inches, climbing up on the window in front of me. He seemed to stop in place and stare at me. I was feeling completely lost, so in my mind it almost seemed as if he was trying to get my attention. Through the stream of tears in my eyes that rapidly cascaded down my face, I thought I saw him stretch out his little arm as if giving me the high sign, saying everything is going to be alright. I called Jeff over and together we watched this tiny little amphibian seemingly try to communicate with me. I had the eeriest feeling that it was my Dad's spirit encouraging me to NEVER give in.

Journal Entry July 19, 2007
Made appointment with surgeon for 2 weeks from now. CAN'T WAIT! Ha Ha. Had to hook up to TPN early since I have to go to the hospital for ultrasound in a.m. Very agitated tonight. New meds, more stress, more complications, just what I need.
O.K. that's it!!!! I have had enough of this S—T. Time to get better, time to see progress. I need to get well and be healthy and have a life again. I look out at my garden and

see all the hard work I have put in to it, and want to get to enjoy it all again. I want to eat food. I want to play with Charlie and Maurice, and ride my bike, and take long walks along the river with JR. I want to go to Maine and listen to the loons sing their oh-so-melodious songs. Oh boy, am I feeling sorry for myself tonight. I am hurting so much and I am so tired. Tests, hospitals, doctors, medications, needles, pain, ENOUGH ALREADY!!!!!!

Journal Entry July 20, 2007
Decided to let a friend visit who had been asking for several weeks now. Have not wanted to see anyone, but she is being insistent.
A good day. Enjoyed the company. I am glad I gave in. Short visit, just right.
Jason called and said he was coming up this weekend. Can't wait to see him. Thank goodness for this day, I am so grateful.

Journal Entry July 21, 2007
A good day for a change. Beautiful outside. Jason visiting. Had those ripping pains in my abdomen and chest a lot today. How do I get through them??
Walked the garden, took some photos capturing all the beautiful flowers and butterflies. I am grateful for this day. Spent time with Jason. The best day in a very long time.

Journal Entry July 24, 2007
Blood test results not great. I just don't know what to think anymore. How am I going to get well?? I am feeling positive that something good will come soon. It just has to! I will not allow myself to let this get the best of me. So difficult to believe that no one in the medical profession can figure this out.

I hope and pray there is some help for me and that it comes soon. This has been a very long siege and so very difficult. I need to get well and be able to eat, play, and live. So much

I have yet to do and experience. I feel so sad and terrified sometimes. Well, enough of that! I WILL be well and I WILL get to enjoy my life again, our lives. Me, JR, Jason, Charlie and Maurice. PLEASE, PLEASE, PLEASE!!!!!!!!!!!!!!!!!

Next week seeing Dr. L. and the surgeon Dr. A. I hope they can arrive at some positive answers and resolutions.

Journal Entry July 27, 2007
Very tired today. Have not slept much the past few nights because the alarm on the battery pack for TPN has gone off every night.

I hate what I have become, what has become of me. I am grateful for the beauty in life, my garden, the birds, and butterflies. Mostly for my wonderful husband who truly is the best person on earth. I just wish we could enjoy this time in our lives. It would have been so grand, retirement, and all. I am so depressed, sometimes I can handle it but today it is tough. Denial is quite the tool, but sometimes the heartache and tears just overwhelm me.

Jason of course, I am so very proud of him as a human being. I am happy he knows how to live right and enjoy life. My pups are such a joy to me always. They give me so much love. I wish I could play with them.

I am truly terrified of what is ahead of me. I can only pray I can be helped and get to live my life as a well person. I just cannot believe the last 6 months. It all happened so fast and went downhill from there. Faith is a funny thing. I wish mine can be renewed because it is gone, gone, gone! Sometimes I just want to scream and lose control, but I cannot. I will not! I am trying so hard to keep it together. My fears and frustration are so all consuming.

126

Journal Entry July 29, 2007
Already tearing up today. Thinking about what will be this week with the new surgeon. Hoping for a good course of action. I need positive things to start happening.

JR is with me all the way and is wonderful, but this is a very lonely time. No one can fully understand or feel what I feel. How devastating this whole thing is and I would not expect anyone to. I keep thinking back to when my mom was so sick many years ago. She was in the hospital for over a year, lost all of her hair, the docs gave up on her saying she was not going to make it through, but she did and we just celebrated her 90th birthday. I must have hope that I will get through this. I must!!

Really missing food these days. I didn't for a long while but now feel very hungry a lot.

Tomorrow is our 35th anniversary and I wish we could celebrate but will have to put it off for a while. Will have to do something truly outrageous and decadent as soon as we are able.
Where I keep putting all of these emotions is beyond my comprehension. The only true relief I seem to get is when the Ativan kicks in and I am able to sleep for a few hours.

I hope and pray that I will get through this and be okay so we can enjoy our lives once again. I just have to keep it together for now.

Journal Entry July 30, 2007
Our 35th anniversary. We exchanged beautiful and loving thoughts to each other. Today should be such a special day with us celebrating in some big way. Yet today my feelings are of being terrified, sad, fearful, and as low as can be. My celebration will be to get well and be fixed. I am starving in every sense of the word. My heart and spirit ache for life. To spend our days in the garden, on a walk, on bikes, at the

lake, playing, traveling, just being together without tubes, drugs, contraptions, and pain. I need to get stronger and beat this.

Off to NYC to the docs tomorrow. GOOD LUCK me.

<u>Journal Entry</u> July 31, 2007
Up early to NYC today. Saw Dr. L. and Dr. A. Jason met us at NY Hospital to be part of the consultation. No one could ever ask for a better child. He is so loving and supportive. Surgery will happen but I don't know how extensive yet. Time will tell. Both docs want to do an endoscopy as a team to get a better idea of what's what. The old enigma wrapped in a conundrum syndrome. Everyone baffled by my situation.

<u>Journal Entry</u> August 1, 2007
Where did the summer go? I missed winter, spring, and now summer. I am still having a hard time comprehending this entire thing. Six months of absolute HELL! And unfortunately it might get worse before it gets better from the surgery. I do hope and pray it will get better. I hope these docs know what they are doing. Having faith, wow that is a tough thing for me.

Endoscopy scheduled for August 13. I have to tell the docs to make sure they check my stomach also because I still remain certain it is not my esophagus that is the problem this time. One day at a time. If I can be well after all of this, it will be worth it. PLEASE, PLEASE let it be so. Dare I hope?
Pain level tolerable. Coping fairly well today, no tears for a change.
Tomorrow echocardiogram and new TPN formula.
Hopefully more calories so I can gain some weight before surgery. Must stay positive, no use otherwise. There will be other times closer to surgery to get emotional, but hopefully it will all be okay and I WILL get better.

128

My family has been beyond incredible. JR has truly been wonderful. He is my rock, my support, my everything. There is no one else on earth I would rather have as my life partner. I love him deeply, and I know he loves me. We have to get through this and then really start living our lives to the MAX. That is a must!

My darling son Jason, well, there are no words to adequately express my feelings for him. He is constantly there for me in every way possible. If there is such a thing as dual soul mates Jason and JR are mine. My mom has been unbelievable too. Always sending me love and support and encouragement. She is an extraordinary woman. My beautiful treasured pups Charlie and Maurice, wow, they too are pure joy and love. Always there for me at my bedside with paws up on the mattress, licking my face, helping me get through this. As much as I say I must have done something awful in another life to be as punished as I am, in some other life, I must have done something wonderful to be blessed with my family. Thank you all from my heart.

Journal Entry August 2, 2007
Went for echo cardiogram. Hope it is ok.

Journal Entry August 3, 2007
Great news today. NOT! The echo shows a large mass in
my heart. Could be a tumor or a blood clot possibly from the
PICC line. Can it get any worse than that? Wow, someone
"up there" or should I say "down there" is punishing me for
something really bad. Now heart takes priority over
surgery. Have to check into what the diagnosis is with
other tests. Yipeeeeee!
I am nowhere near ready to check out. There is way too
much life left in me. I am terrified. Trying to stay strong
but at the moment not having an easy time, sinking into a
morass.

Anguish, pain, resentment, rage, frustration, fear, need to
be turned into positive energy that can be used to fuel a
positive healthy life. I need to convert all the negative
feelings, those destructive forces, into positive energy. In
other words I have MILES to go before I sleep.
Journal entry August 7, 2007
Had appointment with cardiac surgeon today who after
more extensive testing feels I have several problems with
my heart. I have an aneurism, a defect in my heart, and
also a blood clot probably caused by the PICC line.
I am really past my breaking point today. Don't know how
much more I can take. Feeling numb. Need to go to that
place where I don't think about what is going on. Beyond
scared. I need to be numb or I will break.
They are saying I need to go on blood thinners, but on the
other hand, that is not possible because I am anemic. They
don't know if I can go through the thoracotomy now because
I may need cardiac surgery. They may need to take the
PICC line out and install a feeding tube in my stomach to

feed me. No one knows what to do. It is very unsettling to say the least.

Jason called several times today. His support is paramount to me. He keeps me sane and grounded and makes me feel so loved. I have so much to live for so I MUST continue to fight.

My mom has been stellar! A true rock of support and love. I am so proud of her and feel so much love from her. She is truly amazing and awesome. She, too, keeps me going with her pearls of wisdom and constant support. I am so blessed and need to keep remembering that.

Journal Entry August 9, 2007
How do I break this spell of the absolute HELL I am in! Despair, depression, I don't even know what words could describe the muck and mire of the abyss I have fallen into. I imagine a massive hole in front of me, and I don't know how to get across to the other side. Every time I allow myself to feel positive and hopeful, some new crisis occurs. This heart problem, whatever it is, has just turned me upside down. I was barely coping with the myriad of other problems. Why is it that no one can ever figure out what is wrong with me? Why does everything have to be so convoluted and uninterpretable? I guess I truly must be from another planet. My faith is so far gone. I wish I could get it back. JR says not to give up on life. Well I don't, but it certainly seems that life has given up on me with a vengeance. So much fear that has numbed me to the core. Hopelessness keeps creeping in and taking over. I need something positive to happen so I can believe again, so I can feel again. I want to live and function and feel the good feelings in life again. Happiness, joy, laughter. It has been too long without those feelings. Now all I look forward to is Ativan to numb me further. I need to believe again that I can beat this and get stronger, but I need my soul and my spirit to have faith. How do I do this? I am at the lowest of the low, I need to claw my way up somehow. I need that little spark that always seems to keep me going, but the fuel has run so

131

low I hope there is enough.

Journal Entry August 11, 2007
Jason home. He and JR are preparing their dinner while I
stay in my bedroom. Everything sounds and smells so
wonderful. I am starved. I want to eat, more than anything
I have ever wanted in my life. My mouth is watering,
wanting to taste flavors again. I don't know how I do this.
Denial, denial, denial. If I let myself really feel this, I will
be lost forever. I want to cry and scream and just lose all
control but I cannot. Nothing will be accomplished, and I
don't want to upset the guys. I must keep a stiff upper lip
and endure this NON – LIFE.

Journal Entry August 17, 2007
Saw cardiology surgeon and he feels my cardiac problems
are not as critical as my gastro problems. For now I should
be checked every couple of months and go ahead with the
thoracotomy.

Journal Entry August 21, 2007
To NY to see surgeon. Reality will hit soon. I can't even
start to think about the surgery yet. It will be here soon
enough. Dare I let myself think that I can be O.K? Dare I
even dream that finally I can be helped and be a person
again. I am afraid to dream, but dream I must. Be positive
self, summon up some faith and hope, and pray for a good
result.
BELIVE, BELIEVE, BELIEVE.

33

Letter to Dr. A...

Dear Dr. A.,

I continue to maintain that there are other problems going on in my digestive tract beside my Achalasia that started this seven-month siege. I hope they can be addressed somehow during my surgery. My fear is that I undergo esophageal surgery and come out with the same problems. As your patient, I need you to know that doctors over the years have broken my trust, my faith, my spirit, and practically eradicated my heart and soul.

I now find myself having to have trust and faith in the medical system once more, that being you and this facility. I must tell you that is not an easy task for me, but I have no other choice at this time. I can only hope and pray that you take all of this into consideration. I am a unique individual who has gone through many years of difficulty, especially the last seven months of agony that have left me quite fragile and somewhat unhinged.

Doctors always say they can fix me or make my life better, but so far this has not come to pass. Physicians are always baffled by the outcome of procedures performed on me. Not usually what they expect, and only then acknowledge that my body and internal system are truly rare and unusual.

I can only hope that you take this all into account in my

treatment and care. Please consider that I am more than a

body on an operating table. I am a woman, a wife, a

mother, and a daughter. I had a real life some time ago that

I only can dream of getting back to. I always hear about

medical miracles, and I am ready for mine!

I was once a very strong, dynamic individual who seems to

have gotten lost through the maze of medical drama, and I

ask that you keep that in mind, and help me get my life

back. I know there are no guarantees, but a little extra

understanding and diligence on your part cannot hurt.

I know this is probably unusual for a patient to request

these things of you, but I am a fairly unusual person, and

felt I needed to relate my feelings to you in writing.

I thank you for your time and hope you understand, and

keep these thoughts in mind when you are doing whatever

it is you are going to do, when my life is literally in your

hands.

Thank you.

Sincerely,

Wendy R.

Journal Entry August 25, 2007
Faith and spirit gone. Dare I ever feel hope for renewal?? I
am lost in the dark swirling waters of the abyss. Where is
that lovely creature in the movie that saves everyone? Will
anyone ever be able to save me?? I MUST have hope.

Oh to be free from pain, tubes, pumps, doctors, and despair.
To be able to taste food again. Dare I even dream? I want
so badly to be a part of life again and not be paralyzed by
constant fear of what my future does or does not hold. I am
a machine presently, a non-entity without spirit or soul,
drifting through this malicious ordeal. I feel utterly and
completely alone.

Journal Entry August 27, 2007
Today is my 57th birthday. Happy birthday to me. I am
going to put off celebrating this day, the day of my birth,
until I am well and able to celebrate properly. Yes with
pomp and circumstance, with bells and whistles. I shall call
today my unbirthday. Just another day to get through until
I can get back to being me. Get back to a real life. I must
convince myself this WILL happen!

Surgeon's office called today with my surgery date.
September 6, not too far away. Oh my, the trembling has
started.

Journal Entry August 28, 2007
Went to see Dr. D. She gave me a hug and wished me good
luck. Later in the day she phoned again to tell me that my
blood results concerned her. Some levels quite elevated and
I need an ultrasound done in the morning. Totally
frustrated. Nothing like more complications to add to my
roster of fears today. Every time I think it will be okay,
another round of bullets comes at me. I must lay low in the
tunnel of darkness until some ray of light dawns on me and
wakes me from my deep state of denial. Is there anyone out
there?? Can anyone hear my desperate plea for help?? I
need to be saved from drowning in this cesspool, this
mudslide of insanity that has taken over my life.

I am so afraid to write down my true feelings about my
doubts of survival. No, I won't go there, must not! I have to
stay focused on hope. I remember the old commercial on

135

T.V. where a woman yells out, "Calgon take me away." I say, "Ativan take me away," and hope for relief from this wonderful drug that allows me to stay in denial, even if only for a short while. Trying to remember to breathe and ignore the fact that my body and life in general have betrayed me on such an egregious level, my body claiming its dismal due.

Journal Entry August 29, 2007
Had to go off TPN early to get to the hospital for ultrasound. Results show gallbladder filled with stones and very low function. Dr. D. changed my formula and talked about removal of gallbladder at some point in the future. Oh goody, more surgery to look forward to.

Journal Entry August 30, 2007
I must start doing some serious positive meditations to help me get through this next week. I WILL BE O.K., I WILL GET THROUGH THIS, I WILL BE STRONG, I WILL BE WELL, I MUST !!!!!!!!!!!!!!
Now of course I am wishing it was next Friday and everything was over and done, with a positive outcome, but I must not wish away any days because every day is a blessing, a gift, even now in this situation. I am able to be with my husband, my son, my pups, and know there is beauty all around even amidst all the pain and misery. I must never forget that. I will NOT give in! I will fight with furious tenacity and be well!! It is time for good things to come.

Journal Entry September 1 2007 -A NEW MONTH
Thinking about Thursday, my big day. I know I am in denial mode but reality is getting quite close. I hope I can deal with it when the time comes to travel to New York for the surgery. I am trying to be positive but every cell in my body is frozen in time and afraid to go forward to the reality part. Knowing what has to be done and doing it are two totally separate things. In all honesty Thursday could be a new beginning or an end, or possibly even a continuation.

The only outcome I ask for is a new beginning to better health and a better life. Terrified does not even come close to what I am feeling. As I write these journals it almost feels as though I am a writer who is writing about someone else. This is how deep this denial is. I seem to have put myself in a cocoon of sorts, cutting myself off from life. That is probably how I am getting through all of this, but come Thursday the spell of denial shall be broken and reality will sink in quickly. How I cope with that remains to be seen. I will have to summon up all the reserve and strength I can, donning a facade of normality for the time being, and hope and pray all will be o.k.

I continue to be terrified of what this next week will bring, but I must remain steadfast and strong and believe it will be alright. There is really no other alternative at this point, but fear continues to grip my very soul and shake me to my core. Tears fall from my eyes in torrents.

One positive note of this week is the outpouring of love and care from people, many of whom I do not even know. I had absolutely no clue about how people felt about me. I am truly taken aback and honored. I have been told by so many people that I am on prayer chains at their churches. How amazing is that?

I hope the words my mom has used over the years, "This too shall pass" will come to fruition, and that this nightmare I am going through will pass and I will heal and be able to live my life. "They" say it has to get worse before it gets better, well I am ready for the get better part.

Journal Entry September 5, 2007 - Day before surgery
I cannot believe that I have been so ill for the last seven months. So much pain and ceaseless agony. I am a shell of a human being, weak, frail, frightened, and unable to accomplish the slightest of tasks. I have become unhinged. I am existing in a state of non-existence, unreality, so unreal, so unfathomable.

137

Dr. L. my NY doc, called to wish me luck and tell me I will be in good hands. Dr. D. my local doc who is such a sweetheart also phoned to wish me luck and tell me all will be o.k. Many calls from family and friends which made me feel so loved.

Well, this is it folks. Tomorrow is the big day. Hopefully the start of a new and better life. ONLY POSITIVE THOUGHTS, GOOD LUCK SELF, YOU WILL BE A-O K.

TO BE CONTINUED............

34

Surgery

The big day is here. Up at 3 a.m. to go to New York for my surgery. To say I was nervous does not even come close. My body was shaking as if I were atop a jackhammer. My mind in a flurry with a multitude of thoughts including, will today be the last day of my life or the beginning of a better one? There are no words to adequately describe my tumultuous emotions. During the three-hour drive to the city I listened to my Krishna Das meditation tape trying to regulate my breathing and not totally come apart at the seams.

Upon my arrival at the hospital, I had to sign umpteen papers which basically freed the facility, as well as all medical personnel from any wrongdoing. In other words, if things went south, no one could be held responsible. I was then whisked away to a dressing room to shed my real person clothing and become persona non grata bedecked in hospital garb and taken to yet another area for the lovely task of being hooked up to a litany of mechanical medical apparatus. During this time I was barraged with questions by nurses, pain management doctors, anesthesiologists, and various other hospital personnel. I think they do that to keep you from having a total anxiety break. Aside from an intravenous site in my arm, I had to have an epidural installed in my upper back by the pain management doctor, for a narcotic drip that I was to control post-surgery. This was by no means a pleasant experience, but I won't bore you with the gory details.

I was allowed a few moments with Jeff and Jason to express our love for each other, along with the standard "Good luck, everything will be alright, see you later, hug hug, kiss kiss, yada yada." I was taken away, down a hall to the very white, very sterile, very cold operating theater, and placed on a very cold, very hard, very uncomfortable operating room table. I felt like the proverbial lamb being led to slaughter.

There were several nurses and other personnel clothed in surgical masks and gowns, milling around the large room chatting about trivialities as if I wasn't even there. Once again I found myself being hooked up to wires, tubes, and other unknown connections. They mercifully started a slow drip of the sedative to help relax my frazzled nerves, which were making me tremble uncontrollably. Thank goodness for little niceties.

After a while, Dr. A. my surgeon, waltzed in like the King of Somewhere, making his dramatic entrance. He was aptly sheathed in a hospital gown, cap, and mask. As he made his way over to me, it felt as though I had just entered the pearly gates and was expected to ask his holiness for atonement. It was all very surreal. I looked into his eyes, which were about all I could see of his face, and pleadingly asked him to remember that I was a living, breathing person and to please take good care of me. I told him I was petrified of what was to come and that I was indeed looking forward to waking up after this was all done, as opposed to the alternative. He nodded and gave the signal to the anesthesiologist to start the flow of medications to knock me out. There was that ever so brief taste of anesthesia and then total blackness.

For what seemed like, well I cannot really say whether it was days or only moments, the first time I vaguely remember opening my eyes, it felt like a twilight of semi-consciousness. I saw Jeff and Jason, at least I thought I did, although it seemed more like fragmentary images and turbulent thoughts floating intermittently in and out of my brain like a drifting ice floe between land and sea. I kept falling back in to a drug-induced state of exhaustion, my reserve collapsing under the weight of my discomfort, being immersed into the annihilating white noise of suffering.

Upon finally coming out of my coma-like sleep, I was again aware of Jeff and Jason by my side holding my hands, but unfortunately I was also all too aware of the recognition of unfathomable pain all over my body. I realized there were tubes in my nose, my neck, my chest, my side, my back, and other places I care not to mention. I could barely move or breathe. Hell shows itself in many forms, and this was definitely one of them. It seems it took several hours of fading in and out of consciousness before I was able to truly understand the state of my condition and how deeply I felt excruciating pain. This pain was visceral, unlike any other I had experienced in my lifetime. I equated this unnerving feeling to a tsunami along with an earthquake erupting inside my body unveiling all its regalia with torrential rain, lightening, hail, waves, flooding, and spewing steaming lava all at once. I suffered with deep pain waking me in the darkness, searing and unforgiving. Luckily for me, though, there was the magic button to press that was attached to the tube installed in my back, allowing me to dispense narcotics to help calm down the violent storm inside and let me float above it all, even if only for a little while.

When we first arrived at the hospital we were savvy enough to pay the extra money up front to upgrade me to a private room. A hospital environment is dangerous on its own, being a hotbed of germs and infectious diseases. Aside from needing privacy, I did not want to be exposed to other patients and their daily routines, care, and visitors. This also enabled Jeff to be with me twenty-four seven throughout my hospital stay, which he had insisted upon. Jason was with us daily, constantly showering us with love and support throughout the entire ordeal.

35

Post-Op

The eight days in the hospital were a blur of pain, procedures, medications, and adverse reactions. I was given Heparin injections several times daily, shot into my belly to prevent clotting. Ouch!!! The narcotics were taking their toll on me, lowering my already plummeting blood pressure to dangerous levels and causing me to pass out several times before being regulated to a tolerable dose that I could withstand. A chest tube protruded out of my side, which was quite large and uncomfortable and attached to a suction machine set up at my bedside. Apparently my lungs collapsed during surgery and the doctors had to break and remove several ribs to be able to re-inflate them. This was unbeknownst to me until many months later. There are always little unexpected surprises that are kept secret for some reason or another. I needed the chest tube to help keep fluid from building up in my weakened lungs. Two days post-op, when the nasogastric tube was being removed, it was noted that the skin and internal mucosa of my nose were torn and badly infected. I had to have several stitches to repair it.

About day four post-op, I noticed my heart racing

every time I moved, especially when trying to get out of bed. Any simple task, even brushing my teeth, became arduous, as I would become lightheaded and out of breath, aside from having my heart pound deep within my chest. The docs seemed unconcerned and assured me this was normal after such extensive surgery. They told me I was being observed on a twenty-four hour heart monitor that was registering a heart rate of 138 beats per minute. I felt that was a bit too fast, but they remained blasé about it. When my heart rate elevated to 145 beats per minute they decided I needed to be started on medication to slow it down. It certainly took them long enough to figure this out.

On day seven, the docs said I could go home, but I did not feel ready, and asked for an extra day. Aside from feeling very weak and having my heart beat as though I had just completed a marathon, I was still worried about my general condition. They agreed with a bit of hesitation. "Cut-em up, shut-em up and ship-em out" seemed to be their standard operating procedure.

On day eight I was given an honorable discharge. On one hand, I was anxious about leaving the hospital to be on my own without all of the medical personnel to keep an eye on me, but truly wanted to be at home in my own bed, in my own comfortable surroundings, along with my dogs whom I missed terribly. I was still worried though about my rapid heart rate, but was told it would settle down "eventually." I was given my walking papers and departing orders, along with many wishes of good luck from my nurses, of which there were many.

The ride home was very uncomfortable, but I felt free and relished the feel of the fresh crisp cool air flowing in from my open window. Those who have never been incarcerated in a hospital may take for granted such freedom and the pleasure of breathing the outside air, feeling the soft breeze tickling their faces.

My home and bed were indeed a welcome respite, and here I hoped to heal and gain strength. Think again!

BOOM SHAKA LAKA·······The LORD giveth and the LORD taketh away!!!!!!!!!!!!! Welcome back to HELL!!

36

Back to the Emergency Room

After being home a few days I felt no improvement at all. As a matter of fact, I was losing strength, and my heart seemed to be constantly working overtime. I experienced palpitations, dizziness, and labored breathing any time I moved. I also was coughing quite a bit and feeling very congested. At first I thought these were normal post-surgical symptoms, but as the days passed these symptoms became more intense. By day five I felt I was in real trouble. The muddy earth appeared to be doing its best to swallow me whole again. I went to see Dr. D., who immediately sent me to the Emergency Room. Upon examination I presented with a rapid irregular heartbeat, extremely low blood pressure, and decreased breath sounds in my left lower lung. My EKG confirmed tachycardia, an abnormally fast heart rate, usually over 100 beats per minute, and my chest X-ray indicated pneumonia as well as several rib fractures. My blood counts were dangerously low consistent with gastrointestinal bleeding. An endoscopy was done. It demonstrated severe erosive esophagitis, gastritis, and Gastroparesis. I was given several units of blood, admitted as an inpatient and was started on intravenous antibiotics for the pneumonia, drug N for the esophagitis, and drug R for the Gastroparesis. I had to be given daily transfusions to keep my blood counts from crashing. I was hospitalized for eight days until my anemia and other problems seemed somewhat under control. I was then discharged and sent home.

I was bed bound for several days feeling very weak and uncomfortable. My heart continued to race, making me feel as though I was going to pass out. Pain was my constant companion holding me in an embrace, sinking deep into my core, extinguishing the last remaining embers of my soul. I was an entire constellation of miseries. I started passing black stools. Therefore I went back to see Dr. D., who immediately readmitted me to the hospital. I again had to be given several blood transfusions. Barely moments after settling into my room, I started violently vomiting bloody black coffee ground-like hematemetis (vomiting of blood) and suffered with fierce chest and stomach pain. I passed out several times. Before I knew it, in a flourish, there were about eight to ten people surrounding me, doing whatever it is they do in an emergency situation. I was informed that they were the emergency response team (ERT) and they were going to help me. All I remember is a feeling of profound unease and a sense of overwhelming dread and impending doom that was rapidly crystallizing into sheer terror. To say this was a traumatic experience is putting it mildly. It felt as if I was about to expire. The ERT were passing tubes down my throat, injecting me with who knows what, and hooking me up to several machines. The looks on their concerned faces needed no explanation. I was cadaverously white in pallor, and was not long for this world! I don't know how much time passed, but it felt like an eternity. The next thing I knew, I woke up in the intensive care unit (ICU) with tubes coming out of practically every orifice of my body.

37

In the ICU

An ICU is a one-on-one environment where I was very closely monitored, and constantly assessed. I underwent innumerable procedures while they tried to locate the source of the bleeding. This was a no-nonsense, life and death milieu. So many thoughts were buzzing through my brain in a blur, seeping into my awareness such as it was. I wished I could just escape from this sinking vessel that was me. I found myself copiously weeping tears of "Would'a, could'a, should'a" and "How come, why, and if only?" I believe I had hit my nadir.

There were apparently several areas in my GI tract that were bleeding and had to be cauterized. I lost a tremendous amount of blood, and was given constant transfusions to compensate. After a few days I was stable enough to be transferred back to a regular unit. Being in a hospital is never an easy ordeal. You get no sleep whatsoever, being awakened every couple of hours to have your blood pressure checked and blood taken. This was aside from listening to the nurses' loud conversations and goings-on in the hallway outside my room. Rest is not something that is easily obtainable. I was gratefully sent home several days later, but continued to be extremely weak and unable to get out of bed on my own.

I spent the better part of 2007 in and out of the hospital. More in than out. In for two weeks, out for three days, back in for three weeks, out for two days, and this went on and on for what seemed like forever.

During one of my three-week hospitalizations, I became claustrophobic from being exclusively inside, breathing stale vented hospital non-air. I needed to get out and feel the fresh air on my face and in my lungs. I also needed to escape even if only for a few moments, from the grief and despair that was taking over yet again. My weakness was overwhelming, but my mental anguish far surpassed my physical disabilities. Jeff spoke with the docs who agreed that it was imperative to get me outside. Since the weather was mild, they agreed and I was bundled up in blankets, put in a wheelchair, and got to spend ten or fifteen minutes out in the real world. It was a truly beautiful day in more ways than one. The sun was shining, there was a slight breeze, and we were able to sit in a private, protected outdoor solarium in a garden that was part of the hospital grounds. For the moment it felt like a bit of heaven, and I was so grateful to be able to have been taken outside if even for just a little while.

I am blessed to know a beautiful young violin prodigy,

a close friend of Jason's, who came to visit me during this miserable incarceration. She brought her instrument and played for over an hour to try and lift my decimated spirits. After a few moments, in walked my doc and several of the nurses to enjoy my private concert. They said they hoped I didn't mind, but they couldn't stay away, hearing the euphonious sounds coming from my room. Thank you, Alyssa. I hope you know how amazing your beautiful music made me feel, and how much you will always mean to me.

After the second long hospital stay, it was beyond torture not to be able to see my dogs. Jeff had to convince the hospital higher-ups to let them visit me. During this stay I was not able to go outside at all because of my severely de-conditioned state, so Charlie and Maurice would have to be allowed up to my room which was of course a big no-no. This was indeed an unusual request and took some major convincing. Miraculously, we were able to make it happen. I was in a private room at the end of a hallway, so Jeff was able to bring them in for a visit easily. This was the best medicine I could have received, and my spirit felt immediately boosted. All of the nurses and hospital staff on my floor were thrilled to see our pups, and came into my room to play with them. It was a good day!

The doctors could not diagnose what was causing my constant internal bleeding, pain, and weakness. They finally decided I needed to take a test called a pill cam endoscopy. My weight had dropped to approximately eighty pounds. I was skeletal in frame, my pallor ghost-like at best, and I was unable to stand on my own two feet. There was only one doctor in our area that did this procedure, but he was associated with a different hospital. A consultation was set up post-haste. I was released and taken to the other hospital via ambulance. Dr. Z. admitted me immediately, and many tests aside from the pill cam were ordered. For the pill cam, a small camera is placed in the esophagus, and hundreds of pictures are taken constantly as it travels through the GI tract. I was hooked up to a monitor for eight hours. The films are then read and interpreted by the doctor the following day. Normally one swallows a tiny camera, but I was unable to because of my esophageal inflammation. Therefore the camera had to be placed in my stomach under sedation through an endoscope. The result of the pill cam endoscopy was that my intestinal tract was bleeding in numerous areas. Miraculously though, Dr. Z. actually had a partial diagnosis for me. I was riddled with AVMs, or Angiodysplasia of the GI tract. Arterial venous malformations, are abnormal arteries and veins tangled together. Since they are not connected to capillaries, nutrient rich blood in the arteries is prevented from reaching tissue, which causes ulcerations. Multiple cauterizations were done under anesthesia in the operating room to stop the bleeding. This certainly explained my severe anemia.

Another diagnostic procedure I had to go through during this long hospital stay, was called a hydrogen breath test. I had to drink a small amount of a sugary substance, and then blow air from my oral cavity into a bag every fifteen minutes for about an hour or two. The end result showed a condition known as small intestine bacterial overgrowth.

Many of the symptoms of this syndrome are due to malabsorption of nutrients because of the effects of bacteria, which either metabolize nutrients or cause inflammation of the small bowel, impairing absorption. Patients with bacterial overgrowth that is longstanding, may develop other complications of their illness as a result of the malabsorption of nutrients. Anemia may occur from a variety of mechanisms, because many of the nutrients involved in the production of red blood cells are absorbed in the affected small bowel. Iron is absorbed in the more proximal parts of the small bowel, the duodenum and jejunum, and patients who mal-absorb can develop anemia with associated overly large red blood cells. Disorders of the immune system, for instance, can cause bacterial overgrowth. I was started on a strict regimen of antibiotic

154

therapy for two weeks.

38

A Diagnosis

I was hospitalized that November/December of 2007 for about a month. I underwent constant diagnostic procedures and was given IV fluids and other supplements to try to maintain my weight and nutritional status. I had to have numerous cauterizations done in order to control the GI bleeding. My weakness was overwhelming, and I was totally bed-bound for about two weeks. All I could think about was taking a hot shower. It is one of those daily rituals most of us take for granted. Being in bed for such a long period of time is debilitating in itself, but not being able to shower was sheer agony. Having a nurse give you sponge baths just doesn't do much. When I was finally allowed to be assisted down the hall to the shower room, it was like winning the lottery. Being able to get out of bed, albeit with assistance, get under a stream of really hot water, and just stand there feeling my weary body be caressed and cleansed by H20 was sheer heaven. I could not even begin to express how incredible this was.

Dr. Z., who has been my GI doc ever since, now admits that when we first met, he was not at all enthusiastic about my survival. In both of my doctors' offices I am currently known as "the miracle" because no one can understand how I have survived the past few years.

Having to be in the hospital for such an extended period of time, going through all of the tests and procedures was difficult in itself, but missing Thanksgiving and Christmas at home with my family was unbearable. As the end of the year holidays were approaching, I felt so sad about not being able to be a part of our traditional celebrations. I normally sent out many holiday cards, but was unable to do so this year since my strength and demeanor were virtually non-existent. I thought it would be nice to at least write a small note, and send it to everyone who kept me in their thoughts and prayers throughout my ordeal. I asked Jeff to bring me some paper on which I scribbled a message, made a list of who I wanted it sent to, and asked him to make several copies and mail them.

Dearest Friends,
It has been a very difficult year and I am still muddling my way through it.

At this holiday season, I would love to write each and every one personally but do not yet have the strength, so I am writing this one note to all, letting you know how much I deeply appreciate the continuous calls, cards, letters, outpouring of thoughts, love, care, and words of encouragement. You could never know how very much it means to me! My heart and soul are filled with warmth and love for all of you, and I hope for now this note will suffice.

I wish you all a wonderful holiday season and a happy and healthy New Year. I look forward to the day I can spend time talking and being with you again.

With Love,
Wendy

My nurses tried to make the holidays cheerful for me, but it was not quite the same. As miserable as I was though, having my family with me, even for a little while each day, was wonderful. My mom was able to fly up from her home in Florida, so having her, Jeff, and Jason around meant the world to me. That is truly what the holidays are about, being with your loved ones no matter where, and I felt so very blessed to have mine with me.

39

Home Again

When I finally seemed fairly stable, I was discharged and sent home. I stayed in bed for several days unable to be up and about, but after a while felt it would behoove me to get up and move around. Jeff had to carry me into the living room to my comfy chair, so I could look outside through the window and try to feel part of the living again. It was January of 2008, and I sat and watched as a wintry blanket of freshly fallen snow began to cover the ground. What a beautiful sight to behold.

I was constantly exhausted, but determined to get out of bed several times a day to combat the daily deluge of my disability, illness again being my formidable opponent. The seasons of my life became long empty spaces of lapsed time. I felt I needed once more to fight desperately to repair my broken soul. I was a simpering shell of a person, tedium being my only source of solace. Day after day arising with the emerging light of early morning, being carried to my chair and staring out at a world I could no longer be a part of, feeling unspeakable sadness, anger, and resentment coursing through my mind. My fortress of pretense was rapidly dissolving into dust.

I have lived with this body of mine over fifty years now. Caring for it, cleansing it, dressing it, feeding it, and pampering it, made me ask how could it take such insufferable vengeance on me? I was once again among the "un-living." I stayed in my pajamas all day, never put on make-up, and wore no jewelry. I refused to look in the mirror, and did not ever smile. My heart and spirit were desperately marred.

I was lethargic and barely able to think. I was shaky, feeling my arms, legs, and mouth twitching intermittently. My mind seemed to be in a dark place, but somehow I kept trying to crawl out of the ruins of my collapsed psyche. I said to myself, this is not me! I know my body is under siege, but come on woman! Get it together! I am alive in some sense of the word and need to reinvent myself enough to get through! That is what I do to survive! But my mind seemed buried deep in the mud unable to function. What is going on? Somehow I kept feeling that maybe one of my medications was causing this stupor-like state, the fog of my exhaustion seemingly impenetrable. I surmised that within an hour or so of taking drug R, this feeling seemed to worsen. I recalled experiencing similar symptoms over the past few months when I was in the hospital. I phoned my docs about this feeling, and they said it was imperative I continue to take drug R, no matter what. They felt I was just debilitated from all that I had been going through, and prescribed physical therapy.

The PT person came to my home a few days later, but unfortunately, I was unable to participate in any activity whatsoever, because I had no strength to even lift an arm or a leg, and I was very unsteady. I also seemed to be in a state of disarray all the time, unable to think straight.

I decided on my own to discontinue drug R despite the doctor's opinions. After several days I noticed a slight improvement in my demeanor. I was less groggy, my mind was less foggy, and it seemed I also had a little more control of my muscles.

I still continued to be a complete mess, unable to get around, and had to be carried from room to room. If I needed to leave the house for a doctor appointment, I had to be taken in a wheelchair.

A friend of ours recommended a doctor he knew, who was the head of oncology/hematology at a nearby hospital. We set up an appointment for a consultation so we could at least hear another opinion about why I was feeling so strange. Dr. T. greeted us, and we were welcomed into his large impressive office. We spoke with him for over an hour, and his opinion at the end of our meeting was that I had the beginnings of Parkinson's disease. He prescribed a regimen of L-Dopa. I asked him if I should at least take some tests to confirm this diagnosis, but he said he was sure this was my problem so why bother putting me through the added trauma of more tests. When Jeff and I left his office, we were both dumbfounded. In my opinion, there was no way I had Parkinson's disease. I wondered how a doctor could be so sure without the proper diagnostics. I was convinced that it was drug R causing these problems, but he completely dismissed that idea. Two years later, drug R was black boxed because it potentially caused a condition called Tardive Dyskinesia, which is a serious neurological disorder that causes involuntary repetitive tic-like movements in many areas of the body, including arms, legs, torso, and facial muscles, very much like Parkinson's disease. HELLO!!!!!!!!!!!! Why is it doctors are so unwilling to look into other causes and effects of medications before it is too late, and people end up suffering more than they should, and are put at risk for other problems? There is at the present time a class-action law suit against the drug company that markets drug R, but it is still being prescribed and used on a regular basis. As the weeks went by after being off drug R, my twitching and foggy mind seemed to abate. Very interesting!!!

I was still severely weak and debilitated, with constantly plummeting blood values. Jeff had to help me in and out of bed, wheel me around in the wheelchair, cook and clean. He never once complained. He was always supportive, encouraging, and loving. My Jeffrey, what a guy! Forever my blessing, my rock!

40

Transfusions and Infusions

Dr. D. now prescribed blood transfusions and iron infusions at the hospital's infusion center to try to control the anemia. The treatments took five to six hours three times a week, and were exhausting. I remember lying in bed at the infusion center watching the drip, drip, drip, of the medications in the IV bag for hours, my eyes barely able to stay open, my lips quivering, and my body trembling. I was always cold, and the nurses could never cover me with enough blankets to keep me warm. Most of my time there I was barely able to stay conscious.

Every once in a while, one of the other patients who had also been coming to the center week after week for treatment, didn't show up and I wondered why. Later I found out that they had passed away. Always in the back of my mind was that I could be next.

The nurses were wonderful, and always tried to make me as comfortable as possible. They were kind, supportive, and always greeted me with a big smile. One of them actually insisted on a hug before and after each treatment, which made me feel special and a little less anxious. It was a very difficult time.

On our way to and from the treatment center, we passed by the Farmington River trail that Jeff and I had often visited to walk or bike. We had taken many long walks there with Charlie and Maurice throughout the years. Winters were especially quiet, offering a serene peacefulness when the snow and ice on the trees displayed nature's stark splendor. In spring, summer, and fall, we had ridden our bikes on the path alongside the river whenever we could.

While on our bikes we would frequently glance at the flowing water as it rushed over the rocks on its way downstream. We would often notice a great heron gliding just above the water's surface searching for a meal, or merganser ducks frolicking in the rapids. This particular section of the river happens to be one of the most picturesque in the entire Northeast, and in fact, fly-fishing enthusiasts flock to it certain times of the year. Walking and biking the trail were among our most favorite things to do together. I could never get over how something so simple could bring so much joy and contentment. As we repeatedly drove past the river trail on our way to and from the treatment center, I felt so debilitated, barely able to keep my head up, with numbness descending upon me. I couldn't help but harbor a desperate sadness in the pit of my soul that I would never again be able to enjoy this very special place, which brought torrents of tears to my eyes.

After several months of going through these weekly treatments and scarcely improving, I felt it was time to talk to my doctor about consulting with a hematologist, to find out what was truly causing my continuing low blood counts. Possibly, there was some underlying anomaly we were all somehow missing. As always, you must be your own advocate, and never hesitate to inquire about all of your options. You can never ask enough questions!

Dr. B. was recommended. He headed up the hospital's hematology/oncology department. After our initial meeting, he ordered a bone marrow aspiration to be done. Oh joy, I can't wait!!! It was set up posthaste. The immediate thought running through my mind at that moment was the memory of my dad going through the same procedure years ago while being worked up for lymphoma. I had all too vivid memories of holding his hand, listening to him scream at the top of his lungs while writhing in pain. It was not something I was looking forward to.

When I arrived for the test, I asked to be given sedation because I knew I would not be able to tolerate it while awake. An IV was set up to start infusing the medications to knock me out. Aside from the doctor and a nurse, Jeff as always, stayed in the room with me. We all waited about twenty minutes, but I did not become sedated.

In fact I remained fully conscious. The doc said he could wait no longer and had to begin the procedure. As he plunged the needle deep into my hip, I remember unbelievably intense pain in my rear, and letting out a bloodcurdling scream before through the grace of God I either passed out, or the meds finally did what they were supposed to do.

41

Possibly Cancer?

The results showed a discrepancy in the size and production of my red blood cells, and I was given a diagnosis of Myelodysplasia, which is in the leukemia family. MDS or myelodysplastic syndrome is a diagnosis of cancer. The disease arises in the bone marrow from hematopoietic stem cells. The bone marrow makes reduced numbers of red blood cells that carry oxygen, white cells that fight infections, and platelets that prevent bleeding. There is no known cause, but MDS arises when one of the hematopoietic stem cells transforms a normal cell into a malignant cell, which may be unable to make blood cells efficiently, or the cells that are produced may die prematurely, causing low blood counts. Dr. B. told me the average survival rate for this disease was about 11 years without a bone marrow transplant. He did say, though, that my results were somewhat borderline, on the lesser part of the scale, so I was only at the beginning stages, and could possibly have more time.

Oh joy, that made me feel so much better! I think not!!! Like WHAT???!!! This nightmare is like the energizer bunny, it just doesn't quit. "It keeps going and going and going." Have I not suffered enough? I guess hell doesn't call ahead, it just shows up at your doorstep whenever it wants and kicks you hard! Once again the rug was pulled out from under me, and I felt there was no place to land. What it is exactly that keeps me going I do not really know! I guess it could be the tiny embers miraculously left over from the firestorm that once filled my spirit. For some reason, I continue to look forward to awakening each day to see the cascading colors of morning break gloriously through my window. I continue to adore listening to the enthralling sound of birds singing their glorious songs, and watching them flit around gathering nourishment. I even relish a dark rainy day when I can cuddle up on the sofa and immerse myself in a good book while a fire crackles in the fireplace. Every day I look forward to playing with my dogs, spending time with Jeffrey and Jason, and enjoying all of the beautiful gifts of life I am blessed with, never allowing myself to give in to my ever present pain and grief.

I was to begin a regimen of Procrit injections. Procrit (Epoetin) is injected into the subcutaneous layer of tissue, which is between the skin and muscle. It is known to help red blood cell production and size. I had been getting iron infusions for months to control my anemia, but now needed this medication too. I had my blood drawn weekly to monitor my counts and determine dosages. This new regimen of Procrit injections was to take the place of the blood transfusions I had been receiving for so long. The first injection was probably the most painful shot I have ever experienced. The nurse explained that it is because the serum is quite viscous. She told me even strong men have been known to yell when they get it. Through the last several years though, I had luckily discovered that when the vile of serum was warmed (in my hand, since it is quite cold just out of the refrigerator), and then injected slowly, it seemed to become slightly more tolerable.

I would be remiss if I didn't mention how truly alone I felt. No one ever seems to fully comprehend what I go through on a daily basis, and I guess I cannot expect that of anyone. Each day I have to objectively and painstakingly put myself in a certain mind-set to be able to even function, though be it at the lowest level at times. I wake up every morning in pain. Some days the discomfort and extreme weakness make it almost impossible to do even the simplest of tasks. I think about the "real person" who doesn't even think twice about rote daily behaviors. I, on the other hand, continue to be forced to live in my world of agony, constantly being trapped in the abyss. It is akin to being in a coma-like state, hearing everything that is going on around me, but being unable to participate. There are times when disappointment and frustration sear through me like a raging fire. I have heard that "in life it is not what you achieve; instead, it is what you overcome." This goal for me is like climbing Mount Everest or Kilimanjaro barefoot, without protective gear, being left naked in extreme conditions. I suffer with indignant anger at the injustice of my present circumstances feeling lost and ignored by fate, forgotten, and placed in hell to fend for myself. It seems to me that when someone has a popular illness or has celebrity or high profile status, he or she finds understanding and support everywhere. Apparently for me though, a lowly regular person, with my rare misunderstood disease, I have become flotsam and jetsam floating in a sea of scum, left to drift for eternity. Since my disease is mostly misunderstood, doctors become complacent after time and give up, shuffling me off to another doc because each one of them, does not seem to be able or willing to take the time to work with me and figure out the best mode of treatment. They always end up telling me I need more surgery, or some other radical treatment. It feels like they take the easy way out rather than helping me look into other alternatives. Most days I feel like giving up, like the lamb being sent to slaughter. I do, however, continue to strive daily to muddle through. I make it my daily goal to slay the dragon that is my disease, and continue getting through!

42

My Photography

After a very difficult winter, and the coming of spring 2008, I felt I had to find something to keep my mind and spirit alive. I decided to indulge myself and buy a high-end camera to help me pursue my long time love of photography. My gardens were just starting to awaken after their long winter's sleep, miraculously recovering after the harsh freezing cold temperatures, snow, and ice. After surrendering their blooms and leaves in preparation for winter they begin anew to flourish with their radiant colors, while being bathed in sunlight and warmth. I was immediately swept into a world of beauty, fantasy, and the majesty of nature. Thankfully I was able to escape, even if only temporarily from my world of pain and misery, by literally focusing on the magnificent flowers and creatures that graced my backyard. My gardens are filled with a multitude of plants, including hydrangea, astilbe, rudbeckia, buddleia, spirea and ornamental grasses, to name a few. Our home is a certified licensed Wildlife Habitat and we have numerous species of birds visit our yard daily, including eastern bluebirds, titmice, chickadees, cedar waxwings, nuthatches, downy woodpeckers, ruby-throated hummingbirds, and various hawks. Every spring I eagerly await the arrival of the hummingbirds during the first week of May. Like clockwork these little beauties show up at my window as if to let me know they are back and I need to start filling their feeders with sugar water. After drinking their fill, they buzz around in a frenzy of intoxication. So much noise from such little beings! We also have several species of frogs, turtles, and other creatures gracing our outdoor haven. I had been exiled from reality and the grandeur of nature for so long. Not one of the principalities of my awareness had granted me asylum until I started clicking away through the looking glass of my camera's lens while Jeff wheeled me around in my wheelchair. I would spend hours a day as if in a magical time capsule, being juxtaposed into a blissful otherworld illuminated by harmonious peace, iridescence, and splendor. For the first time in a very long time, I felt exhilaratingly alive, and it was sublime. I had been acutely aware of my aloneness deep within my soul with a feeling of exquisite awfulness for far too long, feeling the fault lines of the earth converging and swallowing me whole. My new superb feeling of being alive was like rising from the ashes and starting anew. My garden became an idyllic retreat from my everyday turmoil.

By June my strength had somewhat improved. We

thought it would be the perfect time to venture away from home for a while. Sometimes a change of scenery and routine is the best medicine. I have a friend who summers in Maine, where Jeff, Jason, and I have spent many wonderful times over the past twenty plus years. Her place is nestled deep in the woods on a beautiful lake, and we all think of it as "Heaven on Earth." Whenever I have been lucky enough to spend time there, it felt like I was spending time in heaven. While there, I was at peace and totally at ease. This was the perfect place for me to relax and re-group. I fondly think about times sitting on the dock, looking out at the great expanse and utter beauty of the sun glistening on the water, or as we all call it, "diamonds on the lake," becoming thoroughly enraptured by the haunting calls of the loons. I have spent many hours kayaking with camera in hand, experiencing the awesome opportunity to glide alongside these beautiful birds, and capture their images forever.

I have spent many nights lying on the dock looking up at the velvety black sky, getting lost in the immensity of space above me. I would gaze at the celestial display of brilliant diamond-like stars and planets amid and alongside the Milky Way, in awestruck wonder, while being mesmerized by the sound of the water lapping at the shore. Many nights I have been lucky enough to observe the magnificence of a shooting star dashing across the sky. I have spent many hours over the years immersing myself in the crystal clear waters that feel like satin enveloping my body, renewing my spirit. Spending time at the lake has always been one of the most soul-filling experiences I have been blessed with, and I truly feel my heart is always at home there. Thank you Minna for sharing a little bit of your "Heaven on Earth" with us.

Being so close to death on more than one occasion makes one realize that what truly matters in life is spending time with loved ones and enjoying the purest, simplest things life has to offer. As an old saying goes, "Remember to stop and smell the flowers." All the rest is hogwash!

We are all too busy desperately searching for something or someone to fulfill us, thinking that the more we have, the happier we will be. We spend our lives buying luxury items that make us feel better, eating delicious delicacies to sate our appetites, and are constantly looking for bigger and better things to make us feel more important. If we would just take a minute, stand still and breathe, instead of always being in such a hurry, and look at ourselves sans the bells and whistles of life, we would realize that what we really need, what will bring us true happiness, is already within each and every one of us. It is just a matter of recognizing it. The material things are lovely, and I am not saying we don't need them or should do without them, but most of the time all that "stuff" is not going to give us the answer we are continually seeking, or bring us the inner peace we constantly crave.

Unfortunately most of us don't learn that lesson until we are about to meet our maker, but then of course it is too late, and more times than not find ourselves saying "if only."

43

Rehabilitation

After a time I was able to be out of the wheelchair and stand on my own, but remained extremely debilitated. I had to go to the hospital for a cardiac workup, which I failed miserably. My cardiologist insisted I enroll in a cardiac rehab program that I was to attend three times a week. I was instructed how to use several different machines and practice many types of exercises. This was all geared toward strengthening my heart and body while being closely monitored by the nurses on staff. While on the treadmill I was hooked up to a heart monitor that read all of my vital signs minute by minute. This program was akin to an infant learning how to walk. In the beginning I could barely last five minutes on the treadmill without becoming short of breath and experiencing palpitations, but after six months of determined hard work I was able to walk thirty minutes at a fairly good clip without feeling exhausted. The nurses were diligent and supportive, which made the process bearable.

Sometimes we go through doors that mark new beginnings. This seemed to be one of those doors. Building strength and confidence helped me tremendously, not only physically but also mentally and spiritually as well.

44

Exhibiting My Photography

Photography has always been such a joy for me. I can spend countless hours clicking away, capturing all Mother Nature has to offer in living color. For many years, friends have tried over and over to encourage me to share my photographs publicly. I had always shied away from doing so mostly because I lacked the confidence that anyone other than me or my small circle of friends would be interested. After going through the past years of my ill health, I decided why not try to exhibit my work somewhere? What harm could it do? There is a nature center near my home that I thought would be a good place to start. They offer a variety of programs for children, and being that many of my photos are of birds, frogs, butterflies, insects, and flowers, it seemed perfect to display them there. I got in touch with the director, and we set up an appointment to meet. He was quite pleased and said they would love to have a photo exhibit featuring my work. I put together about sixty framed pieces that I thought would be appropriate for this showing.

Still being quite weak and unable to actually set up the exhibit myself, Jeff very excitedly put together all the tools he needed to hang the photos, and I sat in a chair directing him as to how I wanted them arranged on the wall. The show was a big success and I got a lot of wonderful feedback, and many of the photos even sold!

My ego was sated, and I felt a "wow" moment. Maybe my photography would be enjoyed by others. I called some of the local libraries, and was accepted to set up several more showings. I put a comment book out on a table hoping people would write what they thought, and was pleasantly surprised at how many actually took the time to comment. Children and adults both seemed to love my work, and many asked if I would teach them photography. All of this was very soul-filling, and the experience very gratifying.

As one thing often leads to another, through word of mouth I had been asked to submit some of my work to the water district of Portland, Maine, and have been featured for several years now in and on the cover of their calendar. My photos of loons, my favorite bird, have also been used in the water district classes about lake life. I also was recently accepted by a local artist's cooperative as a nature photographer to display and sell my work. I have had much success there. I continue to get much pleasure in sharing my passion of photography, and hope to continue for quite a long time. It is very positive and healing for me in my quest for peace in my exclusively reclusive life.

45

The Now

Not surprisingly, I suffer with PTSD, post-traumatic stress disorder, but I try not to let that merciless and unrelenting grip of fear and despair at the core of my being get the better of me. I live a life crushingly painful at times filled with compromise. I find myself frequently quelling sadness, frustration, grief, despair, and resentment, all of which make me feel like a freak of nature. There are times I lay on the floor screaming in a blind rage for long periods of time, pounding my fists until I am spent and exhausted from feelings of utter hopelessness. I do, however, continue to trudge through the murky despondency that tries to suck the life out of me at times, and make it a goal to never fully succumb to that blackness that tries its best to smother me. At times I feel like a turtle having to retreat into my shell, staying in an impenetrable fortress, cloistering myself away from the rest of the world in order to stay alive. Sometimes the best way to deal is to pretend, and deny, and challenge myself with visceral release and recklessness.

For the past few years I have strived to live as normal a life as possible under the circumstances. "NORMAL," what exactly is that? I guess it varies drastically. A friend of mine tells me it is a cycle on a washing machine. My life is a constant struggle day to day. We as human beings should not be defined by our limitations, but unfortunately this is not always the case. We are constantly judged by others for our frailties, although many people don't like to admit that they do this.

Every morning I try to center myself and get through the journey called life as best as I can. Every few months my esophagus closes up and I have to get it surgically dilated, hoping that it will be without complications. I get internally cauterized when the malformed arteries in my intestines decide to bleed and wreak havoc in my body. I go through my cardio-esophageal spasms that bring me to my knees. I continue to have my blood counts monitored often, and receive infusions when my counts are down. Without sounding self-aggrandizing, I try daily to surreptitiously perform my gallant charade of self-esteem and force myself to truly believe that I can and will get through all of these blights on my life with a shining clarity and be stronger for doing so. I must continuously replenish my reservoirs of strength mentally and physically in order to succeed. I am learning that those people who decided to exit my life because of my fragilities are not worth agonizing over, and I need to find ways to be kinder and gentler to myself on a regular basis. I am realizing that DNA and genetics do not always guarantee family bonding and support, and that a person who claims to be a friend will not necessarily be there when needed. Rather, it is those with a true heart, compassion, and kindness that tend to help make our lives happier. I am also learning, that it is our own heart, kindness and mindfulness about ourselves that make our lives fuller.

I meditate daily, and try to breathe, dream, hope, wish, and believe. I go to sleep hoping for a night blessed by angels.

When I glance in the mirror now I see a frail, old woman and wonder, who the hell is this looking back at me? Can it really be me?? Who exactly am I these days? It seems that whoever I was has been lost forever. I have been left naked, stripped of my identity. Only a tiny shred of self remains after being plummeted deep into the dark chasm that has swallowed the last vestiges of my soul. Going through what I have over the past several years has taken its toll in so many ways. I lost my youth and middle age, and it saddens me deeply, but in a forced act of defiance I MUST continue to be strong and cherish the good things in my life, and I must always look for a sense of heightened clarity. I try to maintain a glimmer of hope that I can regain some of what or who used to be me, and learn to accept who I am now with self-compassion and respect.

There is always a confluence of paths before me and taking the road less traveled is not necessarily the easiest, but sometimes it is the most rewarding. I allow myself to have "feel sorry for myself" moments, but keep a sharp eye on how far that goes. It would be so simple to give in or give up, and believe me, there are those days that I don't think I can go on, thinking that checking out of life and not feeling constant pain and misery would be a better alternative. But for now, for this moment, I try to stay positive and focused, keeping myself on the path of hope. I continue to be the seasoned performer extraordinaire, putting on my happy face and impenetrable armor when I can, convincing everyone, sometimes even myself, that I will continue to get through. There are more times than not though that I have to shut out the rest of the world in order to muster up enough strength to do so. I am learning that the outside of our being is not what defines us. Rather, it is our soul, spirit, and inner self that truly define who we are. I constantly strive to work on accepting who and what I have become, and not be too hard on myself. I continue to tell myself on a daily basis that I am capable of survival and living a life of joy and contentment. One has to believe in the impossible at all times in all circumstances. We must be stubborn and NEVER, NEVER, give in or give up. Hope, willpower, and courage require tremendous patience and

commitment. We must learn to face our demons and denounce them in order to heal and live our lives to the fullest. We must try not to get caught up in the residue of lost dreams, but rather focus on the positivity of what we can accomplish if we put our minds to it. This is me, NEVER giving in, or giving up! Like the iconic Sir Elton John sings, "I'm still standing,
YEAH, YEAH, YEAH!!!!!!!!!!!!!!!!!!!!!!!!!!!!!!!!!"

THE END

But not really, because as Peter Pan said, "Wendy is here to stay!"

More Acknowledgements

Janine Brenn, my friend, your interest in reading my manuscript as it progressed gave me the courage and strength to continue writing and finish the story I so much wanted to tell. I thank you for your encouragement and sweet friendship.

Rich Gravelin, mere words cannot express my gratefulness for your personal and professional help in editing my amateur writing.

Kathy Gravelin, thank you for your insight along with Rich to help get this book in shape.

Jason Rosenberg, my kid, the best book cover collaborator ever!

Pat McAlindin, out of nowhere you offered to work on getting this 1st time writing attempt of mine published, knowing that I am unable to do it myself with my current disabilities. You can never know how much this means to me. You are a true angel!

As for my family...

Jeffrey, love of my life, "I wouldn't last a day without you."
You are my EVERYTHING, and I thank you with all of my being.

Jason, heart of my heart, soul of my soul, spirit of my spirit, thank you my sweet and loving son.

Mom, we have had our ups and downs over the years, but you are an essential part of my life now and forever.

Charles and Maurice, you light up my heart and my spirit, and I thank you and love you both.

GETTING THROUGH would not have been possible without all of you!!!

I may have been thrown, but I am NOT GETTING THREW!!!!!!! I AM GETTING THROUGH!!!!!!!!!!

Enough said!!!

Made in the USA
Middletown, DE
30 January 2017